The Changing
Presentation
of the American
Indian

The Changing Presentation of the American Indian

MUSEUMS AND NATIVE CULTURES

National Museum of the American Indian
Smithsonian Institution
Washington, D.C., and New York

in association with

University of Washington Press
Seattle and London

Library of Congress Cataloging-in-Publication Data

The changing presentation of the American Indian : museums and native cultures.
     p. cm.
    Based on papers presented at a symposium called The changing presentation of the American Indian, held Oct. 8, 1995, George Gustav Heye Center, National Museum of the American Indian, New York.
    Includes index.
    ISBN 0-295-97781-7 (alk. paper)
    1. Indians of North America--Museums Congresses. 2. Intercultural communication Congresses. 3. Museum techniques Congresses. 4. Indians in popular culture--Congresses. 5. Indians of North America--Public opinion Congresses. I. National Museum of the American Indian (U.S.)
E76.85.C49 1999
970.004'970075--dc21
                                             99-37626
                                              CIP

Manufactured in the United States of America.

∞The paper used in this publication meets the minimum requirements of the American National Standard for Permanence of Paper for Printed Library Materials z39.48-1984.

National Museum of the American Indian
Project director: Terence Winch, Head of Publications
Editor: Ann Kawasaki
Web site: www.si.edu/nmai

The National Museum of the American Indian, Smithsonian Institution, is dedicated to working in collaboration with the indigenous peoples of the Americas to foster and protect Native cultures throughout the Western Hemisphere. The museum's publishing program seeks to augment awareness of Native American beliefs and lifeways, and to educate the public about the history and significance of Native cultures.

Front cover: U.S. National Museum, Washington, D.C., 1895. Photograph by Charles Richards Dodge. National Anthropological Archives, Smithsonian Institution (negative number 57309).

Back cover: Moccasins and other footwear from the NMAI collection as displayed in *All Roads Are Good: Native Voices on Life and Culture,* an inaugural exhibition at the George Gustav Heye Center in New York, October 1994. Photo by David Heald.

Contents

A New Idea of Ourselves:
The Changing Presentation
of the American Indian

On 8 October 1995, a group of Canadian and American scholars, Native and non-Native, gathered at the National Museum of the American Indian's George Gustav Heye Center in New York City for a symposium called "The Changing Presentation of the American Indian." The purpose of the symposium was to explore the ways in which Indians and their cultures have been represented by museums in North America. The papers presented that day, and the discussions that framed them, brought enormous collective insight to bear on a challenging subject that, as far as I know, had never before been so penetratingly examined. This book has its roots in that day's lively discussions, specifically in the papers that were presented. I can say with confidence that this volume is the first to tackle seriously an important multidimensional issue in our cultural life. Nor is the robust discourse you will find herein of significance only to Native Americans—in truth, a collaborative dialogue is conducted in this book whose conclusions matter to the entire museum community and, by extension, to anyone concerned about the inner workings of our cultural life and its institutions.

The papers in this book examine the ways museums have presented Native Americans and their cultures, and how these dynamics are changing. It is, of course, particularly appropriate that this project should emanate from the National Museum of the American Indian (NMAI), of which I have the honor to be director. The museum, established in 1989 when an Act of Congress made us the newest Smithsonian museum, is founded on the vast collections of the former Museum of the American Indian, Heye Foundation. From the start, our new museum has been dedicated to a fresh and, some would say, radically different approach to museum exhibitions. To put it in the most basic way, we insist that the authentic Native voice and perspective guide all our policies, including, of course, our exhibition philosophy. How Native cultures have been presented by museums in the past thus has crucial relevance to us as an institution.

We do not feel that our goals are necessarily iconoclastic; we believe, rather, that our incorporation of the Native voice restores real meaning and spiritual resonance to the artifacts we are privileged to care for and put on public display. We are, in many ways, more a hemispheric institution of living cultures than we are a museum in the traditional sense, because our view of Native cultures is as prospective as it is retrospective; it is as focused on a cultural present and future as it is on a cultural past. We see Native cultures as dynamic and changing, indeed, often brilliantly adaptive, rather than static, which is a status I normally associate only with dead cultures. We believe that the voices of Native people themselves are an invaluable, essential, and authentic component of interpreting the past, present, and future cultural experience that has been and will continue to be ours in Native America. And we certainly do not believe that there is any inherent conflict between our use of the Native voice and the standards of traditional scholarship.

Museums in this country have become more and more responsive to the communities they serve and the cultures they represent. Changes in museum sensibilities have come about very much as the result of a vigorous ongoing debate, strong echoes of which you will detect in this book. While museums increasingly support cultural self-determination by the ethnic groups whose artifacts and materials they exhibit, conflicts still arise when it comes to deciding how cultures are presented. Such authority once rested solely with museum curators. Notwithstanding the winds of change, most exhibitions of Native American art and culture continue to rely on past models—such as the use of dioramas—for presenting materials, thereby influencing visitors to view Native Americans as "frozen in the past." As museums evolve, however, they have the potential to guide society in more positive ways. As Steven D. Lavine and Ivan Karp write in their introduction to *Exhibiting Cultures: The Poetics and Politics of Museum Display*, "If the museum community continues to explore this multicultural and intercultural terrain consciously and deliberately, in spite of the snares that may await, it can play a role in reflecting and mediating the claims of various groups, and perhaps help construct a new idea of ourselves as a nation."

⁓

Each of the symposium papers in this book touches upon a facet of the ongoing debate about the curatorship of Native American exhibitions and the changing role of museums in presenting Indian cultural life. As we survey this terrain, it becomes clear that the landscape is shifting dramatically. The most radical departure from traditional museum practice is perhaps best represented by the growth of Indian-run institutions, which have a considerably different perspective from that of traditional museums. Joycelyn Wedll, director of the Mille Lacs Indian Museum in Minnesota, gives us an Indian insider's view of the creation of this new kind of cultural institution, the tribal museum. Replete with pitfalls, obstacles, and triumphs, Wedll's story describes how the Mille Lacs Indian Reservation advisory committee, outside consultants, and the Minnesota Historical Society planned and built a new museum whose presentation of Indian objects would convey to visitors the message that the "Mille Lacs Band of Ojibwe has retained its culture, traditions, and its home for more than two centuries—often against great odds." One of the exhibition themes is to stress the Ojibwe language, and to show how Mille Lacs children learn their Native language and traditions at school. In a listening booth, visitors can hear Mille Lacs community members speaking about what their language means to them. The entire exhibition features bilingual text.

As with other contemporary exhibits of Native American art, the Mille Lacs museum demonstrates cultural continuity by displaying traditional artifacts alongside contemporary crafts or artwork, with the artists commenting on their creations. The annual powwow, a traditional dance celebration, also supports cultural continuity, Wedll writes, by becoming "a community festival and reunion during which members gather for speeches given by tribal elders on such themes as dignity, community identity, and self-determination." Another objective of the museum's exhibition program is to help strengthen tribal identity by documenting the history of the Mille Lacs Band's resistance to forced relocation by the United States government. "Through the incorporation of first-person narratives, live interpretations, and local examples of national trends," Wedll writes, "exhibitions can create an immediacy that compels visitors to remember and perhaps learn more about the subjects presented." It is difficult to remain unconvinced by the Mille Lacs' new and challenging approach, which restores community knowledge and tribal validity to the presentation of Indian culture.

"America does not know how to think or talk about Indians," asserts David W. Penney, curator of Native American art at the Detroit Institute of Arts. Penney gives us a dynamic and provocative essay that takes a close look at the ways in which the "different narratives" of museum presentation can come into conflict, with "the narrative of art history" sometimes clashing with a narrative of the "cultural present." He applies the idea of "master tropes"—metaphor, metonym, synecdoche, and irony—to an understanding of how "American Indian art developed in museum consciousness," and traces this development through very specific historical examples. He recounts the story, for example, of the bitter, and influential, conflict between Franz Boas and Otis Mason in the 1880s. In opposition to the standard practice of the time, Boas took issue with the tendency to depict Native cultures according to an evolutionary narrative that perceived those cultures as progressing from savagery to civilization—"Boas rejected as racist the evolutionary emplotment of human culture."

Penney's discussion of past and present exhibition techniques includes NMAI's 1994 exhibition *Creation's Journey: Masterworks of Native American Identity and Belief*, which, he writes, "demonstrates a plurality of Native perspectives by eliciting interpretive statements from a wide range of participants, both Native and non-Native." His analysis includes a discussion of how multiple voices and multiple curators characterize many of today's American Indian exhibitions. Penney calls for museums to abandon past ways of defining Native cultures, but acknowledges that "the reconciliation of the many Native perspectives with museum practices is not always easy." Museums and other educational venues should change the way Indian people are represented but, he cautions, "we should not be surprised at resistance when we challenge those attitudes with different representations."

Michael M. Ames, director of the Museum of Anthropology at the University of British Columbia, addresses in his paper the sometimes thorny collaboration between museum curators and Native peoples. Canada's 1992 *Task Force Report on Museums and First Peoples*, which called for "new relationships with museums based on progressive principles and policy," prompted curators in Canadian museums to share their exhibition authority with representative communities. First Peoples were to become equal partners in museum exhibitions or programs "dealing with Aboriginal heritage, history, or culture." Ames examines museum responses to the Task Force recommendations and judges them to be modest. "There has been no lack of goodwill and intent on the part of museum individuals and First Nation communities, but there are structural factors that inhibit change." These include the complex social organization of museums (which are often in conflict with the priorities and obligations of First Nations), the traditionally conservative nature of museums (which makes them hesitant to initiate change), and lack of funding.

In his essay, Evan M. Maurer, director of the Minneapolis Institute of Arts, provides us with a panoramic overview that outlines how American museums and their European predecessors have presented Native peoples of the Americas from the 1500s to the present day. From the earliest depictions of Indians as cannibals in 1505, through Theodore de Bry's illustrations in his 1591 book *America*, to the popular "cabinets of curiosities" of the seventeenth century and the world's fairs of the nineteenth century, the story is a distressing but compelling saga.

Maurer argues that the mainstream attitudes reflected in this long history did not start to change until the 1960s, when "Americans tested and reassessed their political and social attitudes." Not until the 1990s, however, did genuine substantive change take place. The enactment of the Native American Graves Protection and Repatriation Act in 1990, in particular, "signaled a substantial change in attitude toward the cultural rights and responsibilities of non-Indians and Indian peoples alike." He argues that museum professionals have changed accordingly, and now demonstrate a "growing sense of responsibility and respect for American Indian communities . . . in the process of . . . cultural representation." As a result, more Native Americans hold professional museum appointments or serve as consultants to institutions presenting American Indian art and culture. I am especially pleased that he sees two of the exhibitions *(Creation's Journey* and *All Roads Are Good)* with which we opened our George Gustav Heye Center in New York in 1994 as "milestones in the changing process of presentation that force us to evaluate Native American art and culture on their own terms."

James D. Nason, director of the American Indian Studies Center at the University of Washington in Seattle, contemplates the nature of indigenous artifacts and concludes that the question of how to convey "the fabric of social and historical meanings that encase objects" remains largely unanswered.

With many exhibitions, he writes, "Indian culture is seen as a relic of the past. This disassociation between the community's past and present . . . 'disembodies' the reality of a continuing Indian presence by . . . denying it." His insightful discussion of contemporary museums, especially local history museums, focuses on their influential and misguided message that "real" Indians and Indian culture have vanished, that today's Indians are nothing more than obstacles to progress. To remedy this, Nason calls for a new paradigm that stresses a multidimensional "collaboration between the curatorial view and the community view" to ensure that "connections between past and present" are made.

Nason acknowledges that it will often be difficult for museum professionals to surrender control, but argues that without Native collaboration the deepest and most complex meanings of Indian artifacts will be lost. Without benefit of "the subtleties of lived experience" that Native involvement provides, exhibitions of Indian cultural accomplishments shed most of their significance. In one impassioned passage, Nason evokes several "key words" that I sometimes think should be writ large over the entrances to all our museums: consensus, accommodation, trust, and common purpose.

In her brief but engrossing essay, Janice Clements, board member of the Museum at Warm Springs in Oregon, describes the admirable and remarkable initiative taken by the Indians living on the reservation to build their own museum. Starting in 1968, members of the three tribes (the Wascos, the Northern Paiute, and the Warm Springs Tribe), who share the Confederated Tribes of the Warm Springs Reservation, began collecting artifacts and photographs and raising money to build the museum, which finally opened its doors in 1993. Their mission was "to help preserve and strengthen our cultural traditions" so that their children could "go to the museum, learn about themselves, and follow in the ways of their people." Their dedication and perseverance, "the product of community support and commitment," resulted in a grass-roots, community-based institution that stresses Native spirituality and creativity. Along with its artifact collection, the museum's permanent interactive exhibition offers traditional songs, tribal histories, and Native languages. Clements reports that "visitors are invited to learn simple phrases in the Sahaptin, Chinookian, and Wasco dialects."

I am confident that as long as places like the Warm Springs Museum exist, Native cultural life will thrive, and its presentation will encompass the authentic realities of contemporary Indian people. The Warm Springs Museum is the kind of institution that inspires us all.

≈

This book is neither an exhaustive treatment of, nor the final word on, its subject. Our hope is that the ideas recounted and debated herein will stimulate further analyses of the ways museums interpret and exhibit Native American art and culture. I think it is fair to say that the contributors' perspectives in this volume allow for a full view of a complex, multilayered subject. Consensus emerges over the need for museums to involve Native communities in exhibition preparation, and for the creation of new techniques best suited to presenting Native American culture. The essays show that in the past decade many hurdles have been surmounted to bring about partnerships and collaborations between museums and Natives. Though many obstacles remain, we in the museum community realize and accept these new paths and new directions.

∾

In an essay entitled "Rewriting History," the late Michael Dorris asked: "How do we plumb a plundered past without condescending, romanticizing, or fabricating? How do we revivify and make provocative in its own right a legacy relegated to the nooks and crannies of museums?" This book is one fragment of the effort to answer these questions.

∾

"The Changing Presentation of the American Indian" symposium, and this consequent book, would not have been possible without the work of many NMAI staff members, especially project directors George Horse Capture, Deputy Assistant Director for Cultural Resources, and John Haworth, Deputy Assistant Director for Public Programs, who provided overall guidance for the symposium. Project managers Andrea Gaines and Danyelle Means handled day-to-day responsibilities for the program, with support from Lee Anne Fahey and Tanya Thrasher of the Public Affairs Office, Melissa Tallent of the museum's National Campaign, Peter Brill, Curator of Exhibitions, Tamara Levine, Administrative Specialist, Myro Riznyk, Facilities Manager, Elizabeth Weatherford, Head of Film and Video, and Dan Davis, Audiovisual Specialist. Terence Winch, Head of NMAI Publications, persevered in his search for an appropriate copublisher, while editor Ann Kawasaki negotiated the many complexities of the text. Lou Stancari, as always, was resourceful in the quest for telling illustrations. Liberty Whittle and Gail Spilsbury contributed valuable editorial assistance. We also gratefully acknowledge the support of the Smithsonian's Office of Contracting.

W. RICHARD WEST
(Southern Cheyenne and member of the Cheyenne and
Arapaho Tribes of Oklahoma)
Director, National Museum of the American Indian

Presenting the American Indian: From Europe to America

EVAN M. MAURER

Though the collecting of art objects and specimens from nature has a long history among the Chinese and Japanese, public museums of art, natural history, anthropology, and science are a European cultural phenomenon. Because our American museums are based on European models, I will give a brief overview of how these institutions and their forerunners have presented the Native peoples of the Americas from the early 1500s to the present day.

The more I study this subject, the more I realize that museum presentations of Native American cultural objects have not changed greatly during the past few hundred years. Objects were, and still are, displayed on pedestals, on walls, or in cases. Various attempts have been made to improve their visibility with better installation designs and creative lighting. There have also been continuing efforts to create more effective methods of presenting information, to put these objects in some sort of cultural context for the museum visitor.

What *has* changed, and is still in an ongoing process of reevaluation and redirection, is the attitude of museum professionals, who have developed a growing sense of responsibility and respect for American Indian communities, and the involvement of these communities in the process of their own cultural representation. These changes have resulted in a growing number of Native Americans holding professional appointments in museums or serving as consultants and advisors to institutions involved in the presentation of American Indian art and culture. The museum's involvement in this process parallels the growing political power of American Indians and other so-called "ethnic minority groups" in the United States during the past thirty to forty years. For the first time, the white Christian majority in this country must share the power of deciding about American Indian cultural presentations and, therefore, the control of cultural definitions. The historic path leading to this change is compelling and complicated.

The earliest representations of Native Americans available to Europeans were rare illustrated books about the "New World." As early as 1505, a German book entitled *The People of the Islands Recently Discovered* included woodcut illustrations of Carib Indian men and women dressed in feathered headdresses and aprons made from leaves.[1] The Indians are shown busily preparing food under an open veranda while Columbus's ships ride at anchor just beyond the shore. Their meal includes human limbs, as the early European written accounts often described Native people as cannibals. Indigenous peoples were commonly portrayed as creatures of nature: handsome, brown, well-formed in body, living an easy life, and having no formal political or social structures. Natives did not own property but held all things in common. These fifteenth-century Native Caribbean people are portrayed as pre-civilized and exotic. From the very beginning, Europeans saw Native Americans as different—very much a cultural other who represented an earlier, primitive stage of human development. They were, therefore, not considered of equal value to "civilized" Europeans. Such an attitude supported highly exploitative colonialism and fostered aggressive and often genocidal behavior.

In 1591, Theodore de Bry published the multivolume work *America*, which became a standard reference for Europeans interested in the newly discovered lands.[2] These large, beautiful volumes were illustrated with engravings based on drawings by Jacques Lemoyne, a cartographer and artist who accompanied Laudonniére's 1554 French expedition to Florida. While finely executed, these images are still a secondhand collection of accounts concerning clothing, objects, and Native American physical types. In fact, the depictions of Native Americans in de Bry's *America* are based on late-Renaissance models, which were themselves inspired by the much-admired classicism of Greece and Rome. These images were among the earliest "neoclassical" portrayals of the American Indian in the romantic guise of "the noble savage."

By the early seventeenth century, artists in many European countries were using allegorical figures to depict the American continents or the American Indian peoples in general. As early as 1620, European artists produced engravings portraying the Americas in images of a bare-breasted, athletic woman wearing a feather headdress and cloak, and sitting under a fruit-laden tree with her entourage of New World animals. This type of allegorical image gained increased popularity in the eighteenth century through objects such as this elegant porcelain figure of America holding a parrot and a cornucopia as she comfortably sits astride a fierce alligator (fig. 1). Stereotypical representation of this kind was commonly found in Europe for over two hundred years. There were, however, other artists who used

Fig. 1. *America*. Porcelain, 1745, Meissen. Courtesy of The Minneapolis Institute of Arts, Gift of Mr. and Mrs. Leo Hodroff.

careful empirical observation to depict a very different image of America and its indigenous peoples.

The most famous of these was Albert Eckhout, a Dutch artist commissioned by the Dutch colonial governor of Brazil, Count Johan Maurits of Nassau, to travel to Brazil and provide accurate representations of the plants, animals, and people of the region. Eckhout's illustrations of the flora and fauna, as well as his large portraits of Native Brazilian peoples, are monuments to visual accuracy in their realistic yet sympathetic depictions of people, clothing, and objects of everyday life. As powerful and impressive as these life-sized portraits are, they were too objective for popular European taste. When Eckhout's paintings inspired a series of Gobelin tapestries a century later, none of the figures of the Indian people were used. The designers returned to the iconic, allegorical model of the Indian, portraying a befeathered, voluptuous woman who looked nothing like an Indian, but rather like an artist's model or a classical statue.[3]

This iconic image of Native Americans remained popular in Europe throughout the seventeenth and eighteenth centuries. It was used in various prints, in the decoration of ceramics and textiles, and even in great ceiling paintings of seventeenth- and eighteenth-century Italian churches, such as Andrea Pozzo's illusionistic ceiling in the church of St. Ignazio in Rome.

Fig. 2. *Brazilian Fête at Rouen.* Woodcut, 1551, Anonymous. Courtesy of Bibliothèque Nationale, Paris.

An interest in "things American" quickly grew because of the developing economic ties between European countries and their American colonies. A 1551 French woodcut illustrates this tie with European colonialism and the role of the Americas in producing raw material for European industry and fashion (fig. 2). The image depicts the first presentation of Native Americans to a European audience—a Brazilian festival organized on the banks of the Seine River in Rouen to honor a visit by French King Henri II. Rouen was a significant Atlantic port and the center for the importation of Brazilian dye-wood, which yielded a rare purple-red dye, important to the French textile industry. About fifty Tupinambá Indians were brought from Brazil to Rouen, along with all the canoes, clothing, tools, weapons, wood, and other materials necessary to reconstruct a typical Native environment. A village was set up where the Indian people demonstrated their "Native" activities—fighting, hunting, trysting, and bringing bundles of dye-wood to canoes that took the loads out to the European ships. Also shown are a "king and queen" wearing crowns on their heads as they lie in a woven hammock, a Native American technological innovation quickly adopted by the Europeans.

Economic motives contributed to Europeans' interest in North American Indians, especially the Inuit from Newfoundland and the far northern Atlantic coast. An early example of this fascination can be seen in the work of Dionyse Settle, who made woodcut illustrations for an English book on contemporary sixteenth-century voyages to the Newfoundland area.[4] The

Fig. 3. Ole Worm's Museum at Copenhagen. Engraving, illustration from *Museum Wormianum*, Leyden, 1653. Courtesy of the British Library.

book features the exploits of Sir Martin Frobisher, a principal figure in late sixteenth-century British exploration of North America. The Grand Banks fisheries off the Newfoundland coast played an important role in the British economy because of their cod, which could be salted and sold for later consumption or used as a valuable trade item. In 1577, Frobisher brought a group of Baffin Island Inuits to England to promote his voyages. Settle's illustrations show Inuit people in the Bristol harbor wearing traditional skin garments and demonstrating activities such as hunting ducks from a kayak using a spear and atlatl. Men, women, and children wearing traditional Inuit fur and leather clothing are also shown in this scene, along with Native tents and even a dogsled set up on the shore. These Baffin Island Inuits died from European diseases before they could return home.

Perhaps the earliest "museum" presentations of American Indian objects in Europe were the popular collections of natural and man-made items called "cabinets of curiosities." These were usually private collections assembled by rich merchants or noblemen with an interest in natural history and a world that was rapidly expanding. One of the best-known of these was created in 1633 by Ole Worm, a distinguished naturalist who collected objects on his own voyages and from sailors and travelers. A contemporary engraving shows his exhibition room in Copenhagen, Denmark, in which he displayed a wide range of natural history objects, including shells, horns, animal skeletons, and stuffed animals (fig. 3). Many of these specimens are from the Americas, like the stuffed polar bear hanging from the ceiling and the armadillo displayed on a wall. These were called "natural curiosities"—strange and unusual things from nature. Worm was also interested in what were known as "artificial curiosities," or objects made by people in far-off regions. Many Inuit objects are shown in Worm's museum, including a complete outfit of furs and leather displayed on a mannequin, and another Inuit hide parka hung on a wall. An elegant hide kayak hung from the ceiling, as did a variety of bows, arrows, spears, and paddles. Worm also followed a Linnaean impulse to classify his collections according to the belief that ordering the world leads to knowledge and understanding. He used what are some of the earliest examples of museum labels as part of his attempt to structure the display.

European interest in Native American cultures continued through the eighteenth century and is best exemplified by the cabinet of curiosities originally established by French King Henri IV in the fourteenth century and eventually incorporated into the Musée de l'Homme. Located in the Tuileries Palace adjacent to the Louvre in Paris, this collection was added to by later monarchs. By the seventeenth century, many of the American Indian objects brought back from northeastern Canada by Champlain and other French explorers found their way into the collection. In the 1770s, the Marquis de Sérent, tutor to the children of the royal family, was asked to create another "scientific cabinet," where the royal children could learn about nature and the indigenous inhabitants of France's colonies. The collection included decorated clothing and an especially fine group of painted-hide robes, which were put on display at the Hotel de Sérent in Versailles, just outside Paris. After the French Revolution at the close of the eighteenth century, the collection was confiscated by the Republic, and the American Indian objects were sent, with the intention of instructing the people, to the former Royal Palace of Versailles, where they were viewed by the public for the first time. Contemporary sources reported that the display of objects from "Canadian savages" attracted crowds of visitors. In 1796 these and similar collections formed by nobles throughout France were gathered together in the Bibliothèque Nationale's cabinet of antiquities. This collection became the nucleus of the Trocadero Museum, now known as the Musée de l'Homme.

The exhibition of "exotic colonials" and their way of life continued to be a popular attraction for Europeans and Euro-Americans alike. Three hundred years after the Brazilian festival, the appeal of Native cultural materials found its greatest expression in the enormous nineteenth-century world's fairs. Today this appeal has reached new technological heights, with permanent expositions like Walt Disney World's Epcot Center, with its World Showcase, featuring experiences in eleven nations.

By the nineteenth century, England, France, Germany, and Holland had widespread colonial systems and commercial, economic, political, and military spheres of influence throughout the world. Scientific advances, technology, and speed of travel made a world economy possible and profitable. In 1851, at the height of the Industrial Revolution, the first world's fair was organized in London. An enormous iron-and-glass exhibition hall known as the Crystal Palace was erected, along with other buildings, to house thousands of exhibits from all over the world. Everyone, from British working-class families to Queen Victoria and thousands of foreign guests, made repeated visits to experience the extraordinary richness of the international exhibitions.

Native peoples of North America were featured in the Canadian section of the exposition. A guidebook described a selection of objects as being made by "Canadian savages" and noted their contrast to products of English civilization. These persistent colonialist attitudes influenced the presentation of Native Americans and their cultures, showing them to be of less value than their European counterparts.

International expositions were also held in many other European capitals, most notably in Paris. In the Paris Universal Exposition of 1867, growing interest in ancient American cultures was expressed by a large-scale replica of the main temple pyramid of Xochicalco, an important eighth- and ninth-century religious building in Cuernavaca, Morelos State, Mexico. This edifice, erected as an outdoor attraction on the fairgrounds, was part of the official contribution of the Mexican government and demonstrated its pride in Mexico's Indian heritage. The pyramid was accompanied by other displays of ancient and historic Indian art and artifacts, which were received with great interest by the large European audiences that attended the fair.

One of the greatest world's fairs, and certainly the most important to be held in the United States, was the Chicago World's Columbian Exposition of 1893. The Columbian Exposition marked the four-hundredth anniversary of Columbus's first voyage to North America and was an event of gigantic proportions. A city of huge, gleaming white neoclassical palaces was constructed from iron frames covered with a white stuccolike material that simulated marble. This great "White City" was the largest of the world's fairs since the Crystal Palace of 1851. Massive beaux-arts and neoclassical structures were set up on the fairgrounds at the edge of Lake Michigan on the south side of Chicago. Buildings, broad avenues, parks, and lagoons covered hundreds of acres. Individual buildings were devoted to international expositions of industry, agriculture, forestry, mining, and the liberal arts. There were pavilions from every state in the Union and from more than seventeen countries. There were also buildings devoted to the achievements of women from around the world and to the study of anthropology. The open areas of the exposition grounds were used to re-create urban environments from different countries. The largest adjunct area, the outlines of which can still be seen in the form of a park, was called the Midway Plaisance. The Midway featured the experience of international life through re-created environments, including a mosque and streets from Cairo, as well as villages depicting German, Austrian, Chinese, Turkish, Dutch, Irish, Lapp, and American Indian communities. As with all expositions, there were also numerous theaters, restaurants, displays, and rides.

Native Americans played a very important role in the World's Columbian Exposition, with greater representation than any other cultural group. A visitor could learn about American Indian life through displays of American Indian arts and crafts, and exhibitions of traditional and contemporary Indian life that could be seen in more than a dozen locations, including the anthropology building, the Department of the Interior building, the Canadian and Mexican pavilions, various South American exhibitions, and the Smithsonian Institution's display in the Woman's Building. Among the most popular features of the fair were the re-created American Indian environments: the American Indian village, the Haida village from Alaska, an Eskimo village, and a cliff-dweller exhibition showing ancient Pueblo architecture from Arizona and New Mexico.

Each building and display approached the representation of the American Indian from a different point of view. For instance, the Woman's Building, which was devoted to the accomplishments of the women of the world, exhibited photographs and sculptures of American Indian women, as well as many types of beadwork, weaving, ceramics, and other traditional Indian women's crafts.

The Bureau of Indian Affairs had the largest single display on contemporary Native American life at the 1893 exposition. The Bureau built a full-scale replica of a government boarding school for Indian children, complete with dormitories, workshops, and schoolrooms. The walls were decorated with photos of traditional Indian life and crafts. Native American boys and girls from government and religious schools on reservations and adjoining areas were given an opportunity to live at the fair to show visitors what their daily lives were like at these centers of education and re-acculturation.

The largest collection of Native American displays was in the anthropology building. Architectural models, photographs, maps, didactic information, and actual Indian objects were used to present aspects of Native American life in the major geographical regions of the continent. These displays included a review of culture in the Southwest from earliest prehistoric times up to the late nineteenth century. Exhibitions in this building also featured mannequins dressed in traditional clothing, and statues of famous Indian leaders. Hundreds of Native American men, women, and children worked as guides dressed in Native clothing in the popular Indian villages and other exhibition areas. Talented Native American artists were also employed to demonstrate traditional Indian arts and crafts.

Many of the Indian objects exhibited at these international fairs were later donated to public ethnographic museums. These objects helped form the nucleus of many of the world's great Native American collections. Thus, there is a direct link between the European tradition of world's fairs displaying peoples and objects from Native American cultures and the establishment of the first museums presenting American Indian culture to the non-Indian public. For example, thousands of Indian arts and crafts brought together for the Columbian Exposition later came to Chicago's Field Museum of Natural History. Many of the works, like the famous Haida totem poles, can still be seen there.

For the most part, the international fairs and expositions, as well as the great nineteenth-century museums of anthropology, viewed Native American objects as cultural artifacts without any particular aesthetic value or spiritual significance for the Native American peoples who made and used them. The first American art museum to present objects from Native American cultures as serious art was the Brooklyn Museum, which, as early as 1910, devoted major areas of its exhibition galleries to the arts of Native America.[5] These pioneering displays of American Indian art and culture were designed by curator Stuart Culin, who selected one tribe to represent an entire region of North America. Thus, the Zuni stood for the Southwest, or the Haida for the Northwest Coast. His display cases were densely packed with objects organized according to function, such as clothing, games, or containers. He made ample use of descriptive and didactic labels, photographs, and murals, to give some idea of the natural and social environment in which the people lived. Mannequins sculpted to represent the physiognomy of the people of the area were dressed in characteristic clothing and jewelry. Small-scale models of Native American architectural environments were also used to add another dimension to the visitor's

Fig. 4. The Southwestern Indian Hall, c. 1910, Brooklyn Museum.

experience. The exhibition tried to present American Indians in a full sense by looking at as many aspects of their traditional lives as possible. However, the effect was to depict Indian people in a frozen, timeless past without any reference to their present lives or to their struggles with the growing disruptions and influences of Euro-American society. Ironically, while educating the population at large about the depth and power of Native cultures, Culin helped deny American Indians a modern existence (fig. 4).

In the late 1920s and early 1930s, Culin developed a new set of displays for the American Indian collections. The central gallery of this new area—the Rainbow House—opened in 1925. Its exhibition space was larger and presented more world cultures. Asian and Eastern European cultures were found on the top floor, and a "hall of primitive races" that included the peoples of Africa, Oceania, and the Americas, was on the ground floor. The "rainbow" in the gallery's name referred to the colors Culin chose to go along with each group in the exhibition. Thus, the Southwest was painted pink to represent the earth, and the walls and backgrounds of the California region were red in reference to a particular type of tree found in that part of the country. Vermilion represented Asia, and green, Africa. Culin felt that these halls and the objects presented in them symbolized not only the peoples of the world but also their spirituality. In many ways these exhibitions did express a sense of Indian culture, but they were created with little direction or advice from American Indian peoples.

During the 1920s Culin helped others in New York City interested
in the display of American Indian art. In 1925, Morris Crawford, editor of
Women's Wear Daily, worked with Culin to organize an exhibition of American Indian art held in a New York City department store. Crawford and
Culin wanted to show the relationship between traditional and contemporary American Indian art. They wanted to acknowledge the deep roots of
Indian art and, at the same time, let it serve as an example of fine design
and craftsmanship for contemporary Euro-American designers and artists.

This interest in Indian material culture as art culminated in 1941 when
New York's Museum of Modern Art (MoMA) presented its famous exhibition, *Indian Art of the United States*. This very large exhibition featured hundreds of objects that represented a survey of American Indian art from all
regions of the country, and from ancient to contemporary times. Unlike
displays at anthropology museums, the curators at MoMA installed the
exhibition in the same type of environment they had developed for the exhibition of modern European and Euro-American art. The clean lines of the
displays in these elegant, white rooms presented American Indian art in a
straightforward and respectful manner that emphasized the aesthetic qualities of the objects. The exhibition and its catalogue influenced thousands of
visitors and a whole generation of New York avant-garde artists.

Until the early 1990s, the installations in most anthropology museums
continued to use objects from American Indian culture as visual artifacts
to accompany dioramas and didactic murals of traditional Native American
life. The Smithsonian Institution's National Museum of Natural History in
Washington, D.C., had Native American exhibitions designed in the 1950s
and 1960s that remained, with few modifications, until the early 1990s,
when the museum began to broaden the scope of its interpretation and representation of Native American peoples. Like Culin's presentations at the
beginning of the century, the Smithsonian's older displays represent Native
Americans as they lived during the last half of the nineteenth century. They
show various aspects of Indian life, yet have few references to religion or
the relationship of the sacred to basic activities such as hunting, farming,
or the decoration of objects. Painting, beadwork, or quillwork are displayed
separately, organized by media, gender, or maker, with an emphasis on
technique. There is little attempt to show any difference in tribal styles or to
recognize the role of the individual artist. Little or no effort is made to indicate the deeper cultural meanings of the objects. The result is another presentation of Native American cultures frozen in time, which brings no sense

of Native American individuality to the visitor's consciousness, and fails to depict the development of Native peoples and show how they live today.

Starting in the 1960s, Americans tested and reassessed their political and social attitudes. Continuing political efforts by large ethnic groups, along with the influence of the civil rights movement, led to fundamental changes in Euro-American social and political consciousness. Increases in Native American political and cultural activity have brought about changes in the law, including passage of the Native American Graves Protection and Repatriation Act. This act, which also provides for the return of Native American human remains in public collections, obliges all public collections to share information about Native American objects in their repositories with the relevant Native American communities. This provision in the act could eventually lead to the return of some objects to tribal custody. While the act has yet to be seriously tested, it has signaled a substantial change in attitude toward the cultural rights and responsibilities of non-Indians and Indian peoples alike.

This change of attitude has affected anthropology, history, and art museums throughout the country. At the Smithsonian Institution's National Museum of Natural History, there are new displays that differ fundamentally from older models because they include the ideas and voices of Native American men and women as prime sources of information. Through this new method of representation, the visitor can learn about Native American objects from the people who create and use them as essential parts of their lives. One Smithsonian display of Seminole textile arts featured written explanations by both tribal members and museum curators. Each person was identified by name, showing respect for different kinds of information important to our understanding of art from other cultures. At the Smithsonian's recent display of Mohawk basketry, photos and a videotape showing a Mohawk basket-maker explaining her art and its relationship to her traditions provided a very effective means of cultural communication, helping the visitor understand the role of the object within the culture that produced it. This attitude has been effectively continued by two exhibitions featured in the National Museum of the American Indian's George Gustav Heye Center: *All Roads Are Good: Native Voices on Life and Culture* and *Creation's Journey: Masterworks of Native American Identity and Belief* (fig. 5). These exhibitions are milestones in the changing process of presentation that force us to evaluate Native American art and culture on their own terms. A prime example of this is the section in *Creation's Journey* entitled "Growing Up Indian," by Tom Hill and Richard W. Hill, Sr. The rich experiences of

Fig. 5. Illustration of Plains Indian installation from *Creation's Journey*, National Museum of the American Indian, New York City.

Indian childhoods are sensitively and effectively evoked by individuals who lived the experiences themselves. The exhibition combines photographs, graphic texts of Native American narrative and commentary, and a selection of beautiful objects relevant to the themes. The result provides an important new way to learn about the life values represented by these objects we now call works of art. While there has been much debate about many aspects of these exhibitions, they must be recognized for their efforts to empower Native Americans by allowing them to determine how their history, culture, and religion are presented to the rest of society.

More museums are hiring Native Americans as consultants for permanent collection displays and special exhibitions, and as professional staff members. Museum professionals are learning that local Native American consultant committees, as well as outside Native American consultants, are a valuable resource in building an exhibition that effectively portrays Native American culture with accuracy and sensitivity. In some instances, this has resulted in museums withholding objects from public display out of respect for the cultural values of Native peoples. Many Native Americans actively follow their traditional religious practices and have strong feelings about ritual objects that have been publicly displayed in museums.

In the years to come there will be many opportunities for both Native Americans and Euro-Americans to develop cooperative programs that respect the cultural imperatives of both groups. There are some objects in museum collections with serious religious and spiritual significance that will be claimed, and, if the tribes prevail, returned to their traditional caretakers. The majority of Native American objects in public museums, however, are not sacred or ritual objects vital to ongoing tribal ceremonies. These thousands of objects will continue to be the core of the great research facilities and educational museum exhibitions that serve all Americans. If present trends continue, we will see an increase in the number of Native American men and women who pursue academic careers as scholars and curators of their own cultures. These individuals will be valuable colleagues in establishing new paradigms for the presentation of Native American life.

The establishment of the new National Museum of the American Indian and its policy of broad inclusion of Native American voices set a precedent for the future. It is to be hoped that the cooperative relationship between Native American and non-Native scholars and curators will promote new representations and methods of cultural communication necessary for an effective and successful museum. As more Native Americans become involved in this process, it will be their opportunity to lead and our time to listen and be guided.

NOTES

1. *The People of the Island Recently Discovered*, woodcut with color wash, German, probably Augsburg or Nuremberg, c. 1505, Bayerisches Staatsbibliothek, Munich.

2. Theodore de Bry, *America*, vols. 1–5 (Francoforti, 1591–96).

3. A survey of these and many other historical representations of Native Americans can be found in Hugh Honour, *The New Golden Land: European Images of America from the Discoveries to the Present Time* (New York: Pantheon Books, 1975).

4. Dionyse Settle, *A True Report of the Last Voyage into the West and Northwest Regions* (1577; reprint, Providence, R.I., 1868).

5. Diana Fane, Ira Jacknis, and Lise M. Breen, *Objects of Myth and Memory: American Indian Art at the Brooklyn Museum* (New York: Brooklyn Museum, 1991).

"Our" Indians:
The Unidimensional Indian
In the Disembodied Local Past

JAMES D. NASON

Introduction

Thirty years ago my wife and I traveled to a small and very beautiful coral island in what is now the Federated States of Micronesia.[1] Ettal Island lies just above the equator, about six thousand miles from the West Coast of the United States. Its eighteen small islets sit low atop a lagoon-enclosing reef and all together comprise less than three-quarters of a square mile of land— land that was home to some three hundred fifty people.[2] Their ancestors had come to these islands thousands of years ago, and the history and culture of the area are both complex and fascinating. Despite the occasional storm and tropical illness, it was a wonderful time spent with a warm and generous community of people.

At the beginning of my career as a university faculty member and state museum curator, I was faced with the task of creating exhibitions about people like my friends in Micronesia. That task did not appear as daunting to me then as it does now, for a number of reasons. First, the beneficial perspective of hindsight informs me today that the museum profession was then quite different, and the process of creating exhibitions at that time virtually always placed the primary, if not sole, burden of decision-making on the curator. In other words, community representatives were rarely involved. Instead, the curator decided and spoke for the institution, and thus for the community, with all of the authority presumably conferred by advanced university training and professional experience. Put differently, the real significance in an exhibition, represented by both object selection and interpretive text preparation, came from the curator, and not from the community being represented by the objects and text. A second reason that creating exhibitions did not seem so daunting was that, like most people in this country, I had been "around" museums since childhood. My family lived only a few blocks away from the Los Angeles County Museum of Natural History when I was a child, and I found that institution a never-ending wonderland of strange and enticing animals, art, and artifacts. Through solitary explorations, school field trips, and the occasional tourist trips, I acquired a sense of what museum exhibitions could and should be like. By the time many of us complete our secondary educations, we have seen elegant nature dioramas, seemingly endless arrays of projectile points, and the always-favorite massive dinosaur constructions, as well as the delightful, yet eerie, miniature dioramas of whole Indian villages (fig. 6). We were encouraged as visitors to believe that we could, at a long glance, grasp some essential truths about the past. In the case of the miniature dioramas in particular, children could encompass the entirety of daily life in an Indian village of some distant yesterday. These exhibitions were very familiar and seemed, because of their very familiarity (and our uncritical perspective about them), to be what we ought to emulate. New arrangements of familiar exhibition modes were attempted from time to time, but in every fundamental respect the basic processes and outcomes remained substantially the same. The creation of new exhibitions was often a matter of mere routine, aided by a profound lack of new resources to create new cases, much less new approaches.[3]

As an "expert," I was confronted with the problem of conveying some sense of the richness of Micronesian culture, past and present, in a two-case museum display. I quickly realized how impossible this was, how little I could actually convey that seemed important, and how many constraints impacted even the little I could do. One pivotal moment in my thinking about the exhibition came as I considered a taro pounder I had acquired on Ettal.[4] While on the island I had put out the word that I would like to buy a pounder and, in due course, a man brought one he had made. As with all such events, we were not alone but in the midst of a group of men who quickly began to assess the merits of the coral-stone pounder once the maker had left. It was soon obvious that the pounder was not held in high regard. Days later, another pounder appeared from another man, and it was a veritable da Vinci of pounders when compared to the other. I became the happy owner of both pounders, together with insight into why they were perceived differently in that community. As is often true in Native American societies, there was no word for "art," much less for "artifact." "Objects" are "things" of one kind or another. When I sought an explanation of why the one pounder was so lacking and the other so much better in their eyes, I was told that the one was a "Thing made with the skill of the hands," while the other was a "Thing made with the skill of the hands and of the heart." Both were entirely functional, but one was truly elegant.

This was an important lesson, but not the end of what the pounder

Fig. 6. A modern life-size diorama scene of northeastern United States Indian life. The New York State Museum, Albany, New York. Photo by James Nason.

meant, or what it represented and recalled to me as I considered it in relation to the planned display. A pounder was not, in fact, just a piece of coral stone fashioned into a utilitarian tool for everyday use: it reflected the pride and skill of the maker; the role of men as the creators and providers of such tools for women; the distinctive roles of both men and women as creators of food; the host of social bonds that united families; the fact that modern technology could not surpass the ancient effectiveness of this particular object; and the daily sounds of home accentuated by the rhythmic beat of the pounders as meals were prepared. All of these were true and important attributes of the pounders, and all conveyed equally important messages about the past and present nature of life in that Micronesian community. The pounders were not simply "art," although by Western standards well-made pounders are aesthetically beautiful; and they were not simply "artifacts," as we would certainly call them. The pounders illustrated a whole constellation of realities about their makers and users and the nature of life in that island village.[5] The problem for the exhibition, then, was how to convey the multiple meanings enveloped in the pounder and in all the other objects from the island that were to be displayed. Would devices such as contextual photomurals, interpretive text, maps, brochures, or even audiotapes, be sufficient to convey multiple meanings? This was, of course, a familiar problem in all exhibition development.

    Virtually all museum exhibitions on Native Americans face the same problem: how to realistically enable visitors to comprehend more of the fabric of social and historical meanings that encase objects, that *are* objects.

This continuing dilemma and the reflections on it of museum professionals have led to many different approaches to what it is we actually do impart in our exhibitions. These are now analyzed in visitor studies, by educators, by exhibition designers, and by curators.[6] When we consider this issue with respect to the tens of thousands of exhibitions about Native Americans, we can appreciate the complexity of trying summarily to condense their impact on the diversity of visitors. A gap exists between the museum's intent when mounting an exhibition and what the visitor actually experiences. Fortunately, the process of planning the new National Museum of the American Indian can provide us with some insights into how exhibitions dealing with Native Americans have been perceived within the United States. First, however, it will be helpful to contextualize this issue by briefly reviewing the history of major types of museum exhibitions.

Reflections on Museum Exhibition Ideologies

It is not possible in so short a space to review every variation in exhibition type, or all of the diverse ideological statements that have been made in the last hundred years about museum exhibitions, but a few representative examples can provide an overview of the major varieties. Museums have always been about displaying things, whether in the private cabinet or the public state institution. If only because museum lawyers anxious about our tax status always remind us, exhibiting materials for the educational benefit of the public is a primary museum goal, one that confirms the public-trust status that we both welcome and at times find bothersome. Pronouncements within our profession assessing this educational role for our museums have ranged from the sublime to the ridiculous. One can see both, depending on one's viewpoint, in the following 1874 statement by Sir Henry Cole on the role of British museums:

> A thorough education and a knowledge of science and art are vital to the nation, and to the place it holds at present in the civilized world. . . . If you wish your schools of science and art to be effective, your health, the air, and your food to be wholesome, your life to be long, your manufactures to improve, your trade to increase, and your people to be civilized, you must have museums of science and art to illustrate the principles of life, health, nature, science, art, and beauty.[7]

It is hard to comment on such a noble paean to the virtues of museums and their role in advancing national success and even civilization, except how much we would like contemporary politicians to agree with it. Unfortunately, a more cynical perspective about our role today might employ a business analogy. In today's crass world, for example, museum objects might be seen as the "raw materials" that are "manufactured" (through collecting and research) to create "products" (exhibitions) that are "bought" (with paid admissions and donations) by the public. From this perspective, familiar to anyone who saw the Tut extravaganza or similar blockbuster exhibitions with their attendant commercial hype, exhibitions are not just ideologically good but are quite literally a museum's bread and butter. "Good" exhibitions draw new and repeat customers and are "good" if they attract large audiences and satisfy visitor expectations. This analogy presents us with an intriguing dilemma in that visitors enjoy what best matches their expectations; if museums disagree with and do not seek to fulfill those expectations, then visitors will not be attracted to the exhibitions. A major problem can arise when visitor expectations are based upon ideological stereotypes or false notions that museums refuse to perpetuate. In such cases, the creation of informative and enlightening displays is no longer the museum's primary task—motivating public interest to visit the museum becomes a priority. Indeed, this first principle of museum exhibition—attracting the visitor—was effectively illustrated in the mid-1800s by P.T. Barnum's many innovative promotion schemes for his American Museum.

One approach used by museums to attract visitors is to convince them that museums have objects that must be seen. We know that museums should only collect materials that are "significant" according to a given mission statement, and, ipso facto, this should result in only exhibitions of significant things. But we also realize that "significance" has an array of connotations in the real world. This might include, for example, a museum's agreement to accept Sam's otherwise unwanted and unloved thingamajig because Sam is a banker, mayor, and the museum's primary financial supporter. Historically, intertwined endeavors to attract visitors, please donors, and adhere to significant collecting have led to some intriguing exhibitions. In the late 1800s, for example, the Museum of South Carolina's public advertisement described its attractions as:

> Consisting of an extensive collection of beasts, birds, reptiles, fishes, warlike arms, dresses, and other curiosities—among which are: the head of a New Zealand chief, an Egyptian mummy, a great white bear of Greenland, . . . a duck-billed platypus from New Holland, . . . and a fine electrical machine.

The whole arranged in glass cases, open every day from 9
o'clock and brilliantly illuminated every evening, with occasionally a band of music.[8]

This rich panoply of exotic offerings illustrates that Barnum's approach to
museum exhibition was not solely a New York phenomenon. It also brings
to mind the question of how such exhibitions advanced civilization and
national well-being.

Beyond the issue of significance, we are reminded at every turn that
only "real" objects will attract visitors and have a lasting impact on them,
despite George Brown Goode's historic axiom that defined museums as
well-ordered arrangements of labels illustrated by objects. This idea, that
objects should be regarded as secondary to information about them, was
a startlingly modern view for 1889.[9]

Finally, professional ethics and legal principles remind us that we may
exhibit only those materials that we have the right to display and should
only do so with information that we know or believe to be true. In other
words, we may not abuse someone else's ownership or copyright, or deliberately mislead the public. Despite professional interest in this matter, I will
not pursue these points, in part because of both the pragmatic realities that
lie behind object legislation, e.g., NAGPRA and UNIDROIT,[10] and the theoretical complexities inherent in current postmodernist debates over what is
or can be known.

Given the theme of this symposium, these reflections on exhibitions
take on a different character, since our focus is intentionally on how our
society's understanding of Native Americans has been influenced by
museum exhibitions. This raises three main questions: (1) Which museums
expose the broadest sector of our society to information about Native Americans? (2) How do these museums present information in their exhibitions?
(3) What is the significance of that information?

The Impact of History Museums

There are an estimated 13,800 museums in the United States. Of these,
about 9,200, or two of every three museums in the country, are history
museums (or historical sites).[11] History museums are also the most widely
dispersed and universal type of museum, found in virtually every city and
in an astonishing number of towns, making them the most accessible of all
museums. This accessibility is enhanced by the fact that more than two-
thirds of them charge no admission.[12]

Fig. 7. A typological array of Washington State archaeological lithic objects. Chelan County Historical Museum, Cashmere, Washington. Photo by James Nason.

Other facts about history museums are also relevant. First, the vast majority of these museums are small, with annual budgets of less than $350,000 (often much less). They have both limited space and a limited number of paid full- or part-time staff. Second, nearly all (98 percent) have permanent collections, but at least one-third have not created new exhibitions in recent years. More than 80 percent do not survey visitors, but, along with historical sites, their annual attendance figures match those of natural history museums. Third, two-thirds of all history museums are private nonprofit organizations, with nearly one out of every five having been established prior to World War I.

While there are no systematic data about the general content of the exhibited collections in most history museums, my own informal survey indicates that a considerable majority have Native American materials on display. Often the display is the entirety of the museum's Native American collection and is commonly representative of what early non-Indian families collected within the local region. In sum, most Americans have had the greatest potential access to local history museums—museums with relatively small numbers of professional staff who have, at some time or another, created long-term exhibitions that usually include local Native American materials. I suggest that it is these history museums that have had the greatest museological impact on American views about Native Americans, not the professionally created anthropological displays in the

Fig. 8. A classic ethnographic exhibit, titled *Indians of the Canadian Northwest*. University of Iowa Museum of Natural History, Iowa City, Iowa. Photo by James Nason.

larger university, state, or natural history museums. It is not the latter that we should look to as the museum sources of American attitudes toward Native American history and culture, but rather the local history museum.

It is not possible to explore fully what history museum exhibitions convey to the countless school groups and the general public who visit such museums, as data are not available for such an analysis, but we can gain some insights by examining the nature of the types of exhibitions that are created in museums, especially in smaller museums with limited resources. Most of the different types of museum exhibitions were in place by 1900. As William H. Holmes noted in his Smithsonian report for 1897–98, there were two primary types of (cultural) exhibitions. The first was the "geographical or ethnographical" exhibition (fig. 7), which displayed materials from a given region or cultural group, thereby allowing "the ordinary museum visitor to take his studies pretty much as he would take them in traveling from country to country" (the museum-visitor-as-tourist mode).[13] The historical variant of this was the history-period display, which presented materials from a particular place or culture and time period. The second type of exhibition was the "developmental," which concentrated on particular objects to illustrate change, evolution, or types of technology, e.g., firemaking, fishing, weaving, evolving art style, or changes in fashion (fig. 8). This was a fairly ubiquitous approach, useful in displaying historically rendered objects as well as antiques, art objects, and objects of natural history.

Another exhibition type is the "life-group" display, a specialized ethnographical exhibition, essentially a third kind of exhibition format. This approach, called a "habitat" exhibition in a natural history museum or a "studio" exhibition in an art museum, contextualizes objects through the re-creation or simulation of a scene from a culture or historic period. I am always reminded of the example of Franz Boas's Inuit display at the American Museum of Natural History in the early 1900s, with its "invisibly" suspended birds and igloo with inhabitants (which so irritated George Dorsey because visitors spent more time figuring out how the birds were suspended over the igloo than noticing the display's cultural data). The life-group display can also be thought of as a conceptual display because, like the ethnographical and developmental exhibitions, it tries to convey a particular curatorial concept to visitors.

A fourth major type of exhibition is "display" or "open storage," in which the museum sets out everything regardless of provenance, age, or other relevant criteria. This is an approach used in nearly all types of museums; it may be found especially in smaller local museums, perhaps because local associations with the objects thus displayed provide the most interesting approach for the local visitor.[14] Many of the smaller history museums, which constitute most of the museums in the country, exhibit their Native American collections in this "display storage" mode.[15]

There are significant aspects to each of these exhibition types, but given the purpose of this examination I will touch only upon the two I consider most important. First, few exhibitions about Native Americans have anything to do with the contemporary world. Indians are virtually always presented as elements from the community's past—elements that no longer have any importance or bearing on current life in the community. Indian culture is seen as a relic of the past. This disassociation between the community's past and present essentially "disembodies" the reality of a continuing Indian presence by the simple expedient of denying it. Even the exhibition of historic photographs of Native Americans serves to reinforce this deadly notion, as these photographs present a fading glimpse of bygone days, and thus of long-gone people. As George B. Goode remarked in 1888, "American . . . museums are preserving with care the memorials of the vanishing race of red men. The George Catlin Indian Gallery [of the American Historical Association] . . . is valuable beyond the possibility of appraisement, in that it is the sole record of the physical characters, the costumes, and the ceremonies of several tribes long extinct."[16] This was not a random or foolish idea; it was widely believed at the end of the nineteenth century that Native Americans would disappear from our midst both as living communities and as cultures. What museum exhibitions wittingly or unwittingly portrayed and often continue to portray is the impression that Native Americans have also disappeared into a particular kind of historical past. Certainly, the continued use of the pseudohistorical diorama, with its frozen moment, fortifies this impression. In a similar fashion, most archaeological exhibitions distemporalize Native Americans from any national continuity by focusing upon a developmental past that ends with Western contact and the beginning of the colonial period. Worse still, "display storage" negates any kind of educational or historical value by creating an interpretive void within which objects made and used by Native Americans are reduced to a kind of cultural anonymity occasionally relieved by an identification of utilitarian category.

A second feature of many exhibitions is another kind of anonymity, in that they rarely identify the makers of the Native American objects on display. It is not unusual to find that objects are not identified at all, or only by the simplest and sometimes inaccurate characterization as a particular kind of thing, for example, bow, knife, bowl, or basket. With due apologies to Winston Churchill, never in the history of museums have so many displays like this conveyed so little to so many for so long. This disassociation of display materials from real people serves to further distance those people from the visitor. This is not just distance in time or possible relational aspects, but a distancing of reality, for the lack of direct and palpable human association with what we see on display makes all that we see truly anonymous. Display pieces become not the works of the hands and hearts of real men and women, but simply what "they" did. "They" are the faceless unknowns (and, by implication, unknowable), the exotics who were here once and who, like strange voyagers from another world, simply passed through and out of sight. They exist only in one dimension, the dim past, and only in anonymity of the most generic sort. It is these unknowns who are, from the local perspective, "our" Indians; they had no kinship, no religion, no precepts of human values, no love, no comprehension of the workings of the world. Their baskets, beadwork, and other craft remnants are the only evidence that they once lived here, in a past life no longer relevant to us.

What do such exhibitions mean? What do they convey? I believe these exhibitions convey several messages. First, "real" Indians are gone, regardless of what one reads of "Indians" in today's newspapers. Second, "real" Indian culture and life are also past, and their material products are of no more importance than their nonexistent values, beliefs, and perceptions.

Third, there is no such thing as Indian history, and therefore no contribution by Indians to "progress" or "significance" in the lives of present-day people. Fourth, the "real" Indians who once existed are interesting only as an extinguished footnote or as obstacles that had to be removed from the "real" progress that characterizes the history of the community or the nation.

Do such exhibitions influence the attitudes and perceptions of people who grow up in communities where these history museums are commonplace? I think they do—such exhibitions reinforce what is already common in American popular media and even school textbooks.[17] This conclusion is partially supported by the visitor and community surveys carried out from 1991 to 1995 as part of the planning process for the creation of the National Museum of the American Indian's new facilities and exhibitions. These data clarified the many stereotypes about Indians that exist. Just how disembodied and unidimensional are Native Americans? Time and again we heard that, among other things, there are no more Indians—they all died; Indians were (or are) not really human (like "us"); all Indians are alike; there are no Indian religions being practiced; Indians are not U.S. citizens.

It is unfair to lay the blame for such myths entirely at the door of the museum community, much less just the local history museum, and there are certainly museums that have worked diligently to avoid these interpretive minefields by directly involving Native Americans in exhibition planning and implementation. It is equally the case that there have been natural history museums, art museums, anthropology museums, and other specialized museums that along with the popular media have played their own part in the creation of these stereotypes.

There are, finally, a number of aspects to the types of exhibitions I have discussed that should concern museum professionals. Our greatest concern should be the exhibitions' misrepresentations of the past to the disservice of the present. Another concern is the ubiquitous presence of these exhibitions: their numbers and widespread nature indicate how far the museum profession has yet to go before we can say that our institutions meet acceptable professional standards. We know that museums desperately need both private and public support today, but, in the absence of such support, museum professionals must find a way to influence marginally operating institutions. A final aspect of concern regarding such exhibitions is their persistence. Inadequate support often translates into inadequate facilities, staffing, and equipment, indeed all of the resources necessary to produce good exhibitions and other interpretive programs. It also suggests that there is relatively little institutional networking taking place in which larger, better-supported museums share expertise, staff, and exhibition materials to enable smaller, less well-supported institutions to update their exhibitions. This lack of support and networking may be a function of the relative financial stress that large institutions are experiencing in the face of new demands, but the persistence of stereotypic exhibitions has an even more troubling side. It suggests to us that most visitors are not discomfited by such representations of Native Americans. Does this mean that the discultured, disembodied, unidimensional, and largely irrelevant Indian is the accepted perceptual norm regarding Native Americans within our society? If so, it means that exhibitions do convey meaning and aid in the construction of social perceptions, even when those are dangerously inaccurate.

Conclusions

Anyone who considers the place that museums occupy in modern society quickly realizes that museums both reflect and refract the social realities common in their communities. Museums are the creatures of the communities that created them, and, in their own turn, they serve to create that community. Museum exhibitions often mirror the attitudes, values, and perspectives that exist within the community. By the same token, what we learn from an exhibition is strongly conditioned by what we expect to see and what we think we already know, based on what we have seen in exhibitions over the years.

Expectations and prior knowledge also affect those who are involved in the creation of exhibitions. Academically trained curators, for example, perceive values in objects based on Western scientific categories of knowledge, Western post-Renaissance concepts of aesthetics, and a point of view that may assign significance in terms of "type specimen." Objects are seen first in a singular way that emphasizes their individualistic characteristics, and only secondarily for what they may represent. Native American museum specialists, by contrast, regard objects in a more direct and personalized manner that holistically connects objects to each other and to broader perceptions of community meanings and cultural values. From this frame of reference, any object may spark the transmission of stories, histories, and values that relate directly to the lives of the people who made the object. An object may be a representational key to unlock many levels of knowledge and many layers of cultural meaning.

Which kind of approach to meaning is more valid, that of the academic curator or the Native American specialist? For the public that museums serve, both are valid and both have an important role to play in the interpretation of objects in collections. Museums should convey the rich contextual reality of what objects mean from a Native American perspective, just as they need to satisfy the customary expectations that many visitors have about objects and what they represent in a Western sense. Museums need to meet existing expectations while also working to expand the basis for such expectations into new arenas of interpretation based on new perspectives about what objects mean.

Our task is to determine how best to provide the range of relevant "truths" about what is put on display while also altering the "mistruths" that visitors bring with them to the exhibition. Beyond this, we need to consider not only how to encourage new exhibitions about Native Americans, but also how to be innovative about both the process and the outcome used to create such exhibitions. There are no complete, set answers to either issue, although some potential solutions seem obvious enough and have already been mentioned, such as networking our institutional resources. We can also take advantage of the new interpretive strengths that emerge by engaging Native American museum colleagues and community specialists in exhibition planning and implementation, by sharing decision-making about elements with them, and by incorporating their perspectives in the interpretations that result from such collaboration. A number of museums across the country are already actively pursuing cultural engagements of this kind, spurred to a significant degree by repatriation legislation and its demands for museum–Native American community consultations.

What may emerge from such contacts are new paradigms for the consideration and construction of exhibitions about Native Americans. For example, our museums need a new interpretive paradigm that structures exhibitions in a multidimensional way, one that fully engages in and emerges from meaningful collaboration between the curatorial view and the community view. In such a paradigm, multiple curatorship of exhibitions would result in concerted efforts to adjust existing procedures; consensual decision-making at various levels; research and presentation of new kinds of information about objects; and lengthening of the time frame within which new exhibitions can appropriately be created. Other key elements in such a new paradigm are tireless attention to the inherently living nature of Native American heritage and ensuring that that heritage is not relegated to the past or otherwise divorced from today's community concerns. Exhibitions must be based upon and make important connections between past and present, establishing a seamless perspective on Native American life and culture.

In order to create these new exhibitions, we need to find better ways to share openly some of the sensitive aspects of Indian life and culture, such as the important spiritual life and traditions of the community, without threatening or diminishing their viability and importance. We need to recognize that some sacred and culturally sensitive materials may not be appropriate for inclusion and may, as a matter of principle, be subject to community veto.

As a part of this paradigm, we need to create exhibitions that utilize all our senses in contextualizing the selected objects and giving those objects a "real" place in visitors' understanding. That may be, for many visitors, an important view into an otherwise unknown Native American physical, temporal, and social world. In some cases this may be done by locating objects in a specific temporal and environmental setting using graphics, textured and ecologically formatted spaces and cases, and special lighting and sound effects. The context may also be socially constructed with the presence of voice and image representations of makers and users. All of these and more might be combined within the same exhibition, using an array of static and interactive approaches and devices to achieve both emotive and intellectual responses to both concepts and objects.

It is tempting to imagine an ultimate resolution to these issues in the form of a virtual-reality gallery. For the moment, though, it seems in order to caution that we cannot expect to find purely technological solutions to all of these exhibition goals. While technology may help alleviate problems of voice, representation, and cultural depth or context, what we ultimately create can only be a facsimile. The accuracy of that facsimile is dependent on appropriate use of what is available, but even more dependent on a collaborative exploration of fuller dimensions of Native American life. The intricate web of meanings that comprise our understanding of objects can never be fully represented in a museum display. Just as the diorama offers only a partial glimpse of an abstract reality frozen in time and space, so too are all other modes of representation limited and constrained. Exhibitions are, at their very best, capable of only partial accuracy from any perspective. We seek to reason with visitors, and reason alone is never sufficient to comprehend the subtleties of lived experience. We can, however, strive to improve by building on and collaboratively using the strength of the voices and knowledge available to us. Key words to this approach are common purpose, trust, accommodation, and consensus, all of which are necessary for any interpretive success in the kind of paradigm envisioned here. Equally essential in this process is keeping in mind that in Native American exhibitions, as in history, there is no single, absolute truth about all that is presented.

The nature of the best approach to this kind of new exhibition will almost certainly vary from museum to museum, dependent in each case on available resources, including community expertise and the character of a museum's staff. Hiring Native American curators to achieve a multi-perspective exhibition, for example, would not be a universal solution. For the majority of institutions, it is a moot point because of the limited availability of such personnel, but it remains a valuable strategy in the case of Native American "core" museums, such as the National Museum of the American Indian and tribal museums. Instead, museum staff and board members, especially at small museums, must be persuaded that new approaches to the exhibition of Native American objects can result in enriching and productive processes that will extend beyond the museum's resources into the relevant Native American community.

There are four possible steps toward this goal. The first is represented by a need for demonstrating that a new approach to Native American inter-pretation is both feasible and successful. While several museums have made efforts in this direction, the most comprehensive, long-term, and openly experimental attempts have been made by the National Museum of the Amer-ican Indian in its exhibition facility in New York City, the George Gustav Heye Center. The inaugural exhibitions there, as well as the exhibition plans now established for the museum to be built on the Mall in Washington, D.C., have endeavored to break new ground in both process and outcome for Native American exhibitions. As might be expected in such experimental works, the results have been as varied as they have been encouraging.

Second, we need to find more effective mechanisms to transport new approaches and interpretive information about objects between museums. This mechanism must provide for transfers not only from tribal to non-tribal museums but also from large to small museums, and vice versa. While creating new and focused regional workshops using regional consulting teams might suffice, coordination with and involvement of Native American specialists is essential. Another option should be the extension of the vir-tual "Fourth Museum" concept that has figured so prominently in the operational design plans for the National Museum of the American Indian. The Fourth Museum (the other three being the Heye Center, the Cultural Resources Center in Suitland, Maryland, and the future Mall museum) refers to the networking of tribal communities and institutions with NMAI.

Acting as an integrated collaborative, the Fourth Museum ensures a close, ongoing partnership of communities with NMAI in seeking new strategies and using shared strengths to achieve common goals and resolve common problems, including exhibition planning and policies.

Third, the approach to a new paradigm for the creation of dynamic interpretive programs on Native American materials must be founded on and utilize updated specimen documentation research beyond what is customarily done in most museums. Such research would combine varied data sources to yield information that integrates the "Indian voice" with what has been the customary curatorial data found in most contemporary object labels. A new approach to documentation would require collaboration with tribal specialists and would permit museums not only to culturally "personalize" presentations but also to provide layered and interconnected meanings about objects. Museums could begin to give visitors new levels of insight— aesthetic, historic, political, economic, spiritual—into the actual meaning of objects to tribal communities. Given the ways in which many exhibition designers today deal with exhibition text, this will mean creating innovative approaches to information delivery, whether in text or other formats.

Fourth, and last, it is necessary that both museum curators and tribal specialists agree that new approaches to research and interpretation are not only desirable but feasible. Native Americans have complained for decades that museum exhibitions misrepresent their history and culture. They should therefore welcome the opportunity to experiment with mechanisms in the creation of new and hopefully better interpretations. Non-Native curators have similarly espoused as a goal the collecting of new data that can improve the interpretation of objects. But in this new paradigm for interpretation, more is asked of both, for the Native American specialist and community must decide to entrust the museum with new knowledge, and, moreover, to trust that the museum will not misuse or fail to use that knowledge. At the same time, the curator and museum board must be willing to yield control over a significant and important part of interpretation to the Native American specialist and community.

It is difficult to give up control and authority where total control and singular authority have been the norm. It is also difficult to begin with the assumption of trust when there has been so little in the past. But with NAGPRA and other social goals for national unity before us, we face a historic period in which we must seek cooperation. As professionals and as members of society, we need to prove that collaboration in new methods and styles of interpreting our world is a feasible goal that can be achieved at all levels, whether in the context of NMAI or the local history museum. This new idea is still a "work in progress," and there will be many fears to allay, but the example for collaboration already in place at NMAI represents a model for us. The ultimate resolution must come with our willingness to agree that past interpretations are not adequate; that new approaches are available that will improve our exhibitions; and that we collaborate, share decision-making power, and work to create new interpretations of Native American life. In achieving this goal we can help to change America.

NOTES

1. This 1967–68 research in what was then Truk District, the United States Trust Territory of the Pacific Islands, was supported by grants from the National Institute of Mental Health, National Institutes of Health, and the Graduate School, University of Washington.

2. Ettal Island is at 5'34"N, 153'35"E, and has a total land mass of approximately 0.73 square miles, with the entire resident population on the largest islet of 0.38 square miles. The de facto population in 1967–68 was 342, but the de jure population was higher.

3. For example, the period from the late 1970s through the early to mid 1980s was for many larger institutions, including my own museum, one of dire financial constraints. Draconian budgetary cuts for many museums virtually eliminated possibilities for significant changes. Many smaller institutions lacked budgets that were adequate to fund major improvements, whether in exhibitions or basic collection care.

4. Taro-root tubers of either the "wet land," *Colocasia*, or "dry land," *Alocasia*, varieties are a major staple and are cooked and usually pounded into a mashed form prior to eating.

5. This conceptual regard for objects, a commonplace reality within many non-Western cultures, including Native American cultures, has also been the subject of contemporary scholarly attention. For one variety of such studies see, for example, *The Social Life of Things*, ed. Arjun Appadurai (Cambridge University Press, 1986).

6. This point is supported by the regularity of special issues of *Museum News* that focus on visitors and exhibitions, by articles in other major journals, and by numerous new books on this subject that have appeared within the last decade.

7. Quoted in "Museums of the Future," George Brown Goode, *Report of the U.S. National Museum for the Year Ending June 30, 1889* (Washington, D.C.: Government Printing Office, 1891), 431.

8. This advertisement for the Museum of South Carolina is from Caroline Borowsky, "The Charleston Museum: 1773–1963," *Museum News* 41(6):12 (February 1963).

9. Goode's actual remark was "An efficient educational museum may be described as a collection of instructive labels, each illustrated by a well-selected specimen." George Brown Goode, op. cit., 433.

10. NAGPRA refers to the "Native American Graves Protection and Repatriation Act," (U.S.) Public Law 101-601 (43 CFR Part 10), 16 November 1990. UNIDROIT refers to the "Final Act of the Diplomatic Conference for the Adoption of the Draft Unidroit Convention on the International Return of Stolen or Illegally Exported Cultural Objects," 24 June 1995, Rome, Italy.

11. The source for this data is *Data Report*, American Association of Museums, 1992, Exhibit 9, 29. The report presents information collected in a 1989 survey.

12. This data is from the work cited in note 7.

13. William Holmes, "Department of Anthropology," *Report of the U.S. National Museum for the Year Ending June 30, 1898* (Washington, D.C.: Government Printing Office, 1899).

14. This brief outline ignores other obvious categories of museum exhibitions such as temporary or "permanent," traveling or in-house, as these are not as fundamentally important in terms of how objects are used in exhibitions.

15. This is admittedly an impressionistic conclusion based on personal visits to museums in more than half the states, but on the basis of those visits I believe it to be accurate.

16. Goode, op. cit.

17. One interesting summary of popular film representations of American history and Native Americans can be found in George MacDonald Fraser's entertaining book, *The Hollywood History of the World* (Beech Tree Books, 1988).

The Poetics of Museum Representations: Tropes of Recent American Indian Art Exhibitions

DAVID W. PENNEY

> When we seek to make sense of such problematic topics as human
> nature, culture, society, and history, we never say precisely what we wish
> to say or mean precisely what we say. Our discourse always tends to slip
> away from our data towards the structures of consciousness with which
> we are trying to grasp them; or, what amounts to the same thing, the
> data always resist the coherency of the image which we are trying to
> fashion of them. Moreover, in topics such as these, there are always
> legitimate grounds for differences of opinion as to what they are, how
> they should be spoken about, and the kinds of knowledge we can have
> of them. [1]

The last twenty years have seen tremendous change in the ways museums
deal with American Indians. Today, when museums consider organizing
an exhibition with an American Indian topic, there are nearly always three
major agents at work: the institution of the museum and representatives of
living American Indian communities (present in fact or at least in consideration), both of whom address the third agent, the "object" of the exhibition.
More than twenty years ago there was only the museum and its object. Most
museum professionals today would acknowledge the importance of including the "Native voice," though they are often not sure how to respond to
what that "voice" may say. Native American consultants, advisory boards,
and community representatives are similarly confused about the intentions
of museums when they are asked to participate. I remember sitting in a
planning meeting for the *Museum of the Americas* exhibition (which opened
in 1993 at the Dallas Museum of Art) as a consultant hired to assist a committee of American Indian officials from very different backgrounds who
had been assembled to advise the museum staff.[2] As the conversation got
under way, it seemed as if the museum staff and the advisory group were
speaking two different languages; neither group was able to establish a
frame of reference that was meaningful to the other. At the heart of the

problem, I felt, was the inability of both the museum staff and the advisory committee to see that each side had applied different narratives to the collections that were to be displayed, narratives so rooted in basic cultural assumptions that they remained veiled even to those who spoke them. On one hand was the narrative of an art history, ordered by a chronological and geographical framework and featuring the "masterpiece" as its qualitative focus. On the other hand was a narrative relevant only to a cultural present, a here-and-now of meaningfulness where objects were evaluated with criteria tied to personal and community experience.

I wish to address these underlying narratives that are a part of creating and viewing museum exhibitions. Timothy W. Luke begins his book *Shows of Force* with the statement, "Art exhibitions in the last analysis are elaborate and expensive works of educational theater with their own special rhetorical agendas and peculiar political teachings."[3] In this intentionally provocative statement, I want to isolate for the moment the issues of rhetoric, teaching, and ideology. All of us would agree that museum exhibitions are intended to teach, but I think Luke is correct to link teaching with the notion of rhetoric. Rhetoric in its classical sense is the use of language to convince. Rhetoric as an oratorical or literary device is never neutral; its figures of speech are calculated to promote a certain point of view. Teaching employs rhetoric to convince us of the truth of the content taught and the falsehood of alternative ideas. Proper and skillful use of rhetoric, therefore, has the ability to conceal the ideological contingencies of its argument, to masquerade ideology as objectivity. If we can reveal the rhetoric in what museums teach, ideological content becomes visible as well.

Karl Mannheim described two very basic types of ideologies, those that are "situationally congruent," or which support the way things are, and those that are "situationally transcendent," or which advocate change.[4] The large, public museums of my experience tend to promote situationally congruent ideologies and are particularly adept at convincing visitors that they are ideologically committed to objective truth through the skillful use of rhetoric in exhibition design and planning. It is fair to say that the majority of Native people involved with museums advocate ideologies of change, Mannheim's situationally transcendent ideologies, though I sense some uncertainty as to the kinds of changes desired. Most of what I have heard or read has been formulated as a critique of existing practice, or as a response to museum proposals for specific projects. Only rarely, and the work of the National Museum of the American Indian (NMAI) is one such instance, have alternative ideologies such as those from the Native voice been allowed to formulate exhibition projects from the ground up. It is curious that both of the projects of self-representation launched by NMAI during the last three years have met with some derision and hostility by the New York press. Amy Gamerman of the *Wall Street Journal* characterized the inaugural project of 1992, *Pathways of Tradition*, as a "mess" and a "fuzzy-headed muddle" that "blunders" in its presentation. Grace Glueck, the respected *New York Times* critic, referred to this project as a "disaster."[5] Critics are not supposed to be objective, and certainly they are entitled to publish their opinions. Still, I would argue, there is something else going on here. Inherited cultural structures and rhetorical practices are imposed on those who wish to organize museum exhibitions. If American Indian communities wish to employ museum exhibitions as a means of promoting ideologies of change, or of undermining narratives that have been imposed upon them by substituting new narratives in their place, then it is necessary to understand the rhetoric one wishes to wield and sharpen the transgressive texts so that even wizened critics can understand them.

Museum representations of American Indians stem from three fields of discourse, which are often combined in practice. These are ethnography, history, and art. Of the three, ethnography has the precedence of age. Ethnographic exhibitions in natural history museums have often depended on a practice that James Clifford calls ethnographic allegory, which refers to the way ethnography translates cultural observations into analogous "humanistic" categories in order to make them understandable.[6] Through allegory, otherwise incomprehensible activities (if one is an outsider) can be understood as "politics," "economy," or "religion."[7] All who have visited natural history museums have seen displays organized into such categories. Those without some training in ethnography—most of the general public—might fail to understand that many of the cultural events represented in this way possess political, economic, and religious dimensions simultaneously and that the imposition of such terms involves, in fact, nothing more than a rhetorical strategy.

The application of the word "art," like "politics" or "religion," to many categories of traditional American Indian objects is possible only through allegory. The introduction of American Indian "art" to museums stemmed from its ethnographic definition, the development of a pan-cultural, allegorically formulated "humanistic" definition of art. These objects have yet to escape this identity.

The ethnographic allegory of American Indian art was first invoked in support of the early generations of Pueblo watercolorists and Anadarko painters of the 1910s and 1920s. The artist John Sloan, the dealer Amelia Elizabeth White, and others promoted the work of these early Indian painters by stressing their unity with sculptured, painted, woven, and modeled American Indian objects produced in the past that possess a wide range of political, religious, economic, or cultural dimensions in addition to their artistry: kiva paintings, pictographs, decorated pottery, and basketry. Sloan and White organized the *Exposition of Indian Tribal Arts* in 1931, where modern watercolors were shown side by side with baskets, pottery, jewelry, beadwork, carving, and textiles of earlier generations.[8] This juxtaposition was calculated to authenticate the watercolors as artifacts while reclassifying the other objects as works of art, seamlessly joining the two together by means of an elaborate ethnographic allegory of American Indian painting "at once classic and modern."[9]

Living weavers, potters, and jewelry- and basket-makers certainly benefited from this reconsideration of their work; many had turned their efforts in traditional media to the production of objects for sale in the art market. The conceptual change was anticipated and forced by this shift in practice, as Indian people working in traditional and new media found markets among travelers, tourists, traders, and galleries that easily understood the potential for translating these objects into art commodities. When ethnographic allegory merged the notions of artifact and art, however, dealers, consumers, and museums began to evaluate these commodities not only in terms of their artistry but also in terms of their "authenticity" as "artifacts" unmediated by the outside world. Traders and dealers often concealed (and still do conceal) the marketplace orientation of early twentieth-century craft traditions from their clients, stressing instead exotic, tribal, and even "primitive" qualities.

It is interesting to trace the allegorical definition of American Indian art as it began to emerge in exhibitions during the first half of this century. In so doing, I have found it helpful to think about historiographer Hayden White's notions of "master tropes." The master tropes—metaphor, metonym, synecdoche, and irony—derive from post-Renaissance literary theory and refer to the way representations are *prefigured* as objects of discourse, which establishes their outline and content so we may speak of them.[10] The notion of American Indian art developed in the museum consciousness with the help of the prefigurative master tropes. The trope of metaphor dominates efforts of the *Exposition of Indian Tribal Arts* to affirm the equivalence of Indian and European arts and the unities that bind together all Indian traditions of technique and cultural meaning. "The American Indian race possesses an innate talent in the fine and applied arts," wrote Sloan in his opening statement of the catalogue printed in 1931. "The Indian is a born artist."[11] In conclusion he said that "the search for harmony and success within himself and within the tribe is voiced in dances by forms, designs, rhythms, symbols, until one is led from them back to his art again, realizing that they are all beats of one pulse."[12] The theme of metaphorical unity is repeated in the chapter headings of the second volume of the publication: "Indian symbolism," "Indian poetry," "Indian pottery," "Indian sculpture and carving," and "Indian masks."[13] The rhetorical strategy of the Tribal Arts Exposition is blatantly clear and not completely blameworthy. Its intent is to convince a novice public that the values associated with fine art can be appropriately applied to Indian-made objects. The Indian fine-arts tradition is allegorically structured in terms of equivalence to the European fine-arts tradition. It accounts for the observable differences of style, technique, media, and meaning by appealing to the notion of a cultural and racial difference between Indians and Europeans while remaining the same in a broader humanistic sense—the same, but different.

In the 1930s and for decades thereafter, that difference and similarity, the unity within and separateness from without, narrowly defined what American Indian art could be. Dorothy Dunn's Studio School, the Philbrook Museum's Annual Indian Art exhibitions, and other art institutions all enforced the "Indian-ness" in American Indian art, insisting on a narrow range of stylistic and subject conventions as visual signifiers of this identity (excluding from consideration, for the time being, those that transgressed these conventions, like Albert Looking Elk, Oscar Howe, and Joe Herrera later in his career).[14] When allegorical definitions of "art" were assigned to objects, the other cultural associations of these objects were overlooked or obscured, creating a situation that has come back to haunt us now when many tribes are reasserting the religious and cultural identities of these very same objects.

While Sloan and the Tribal Arts Exposition emphasized the metaphorical unity of American Indian art, the early generation of anthropologists struggled with the trope of metonymy when organizing ethnographic exhibitions. The bitter disagreement over display strategies in the late 1880s between Franz Boas, who was at the time editor of *Science* magazine and who later became curator at the American Museum of Natural History, and Otis Mason, curator of ethnology at the Smithsonian Institution's United States National Museum, was, in fact, a struggle over conflicting metonymic tropes: how to divide their collections into meaningful groupings and establish the logic of their relationships. Both men understood that the metonymic arrangements of the collections constructed a narrative. For Mason, the categorization of object by technology—weapons, baskets, musical instruments, and clothing—and their arrangement from primitive to most advanced, illustrated a story of human progress. This narrative stemmed from the writings of American anthropologist Lewis Henry Morgan about the progress of humanity through stages of cultural development, from "savagery" through "barbarism" to "civilization." Boas rejected as racist the evolutionary emplotment of human culture, which he correctly perceived as the reason why at the time mainstream America was so committed to it. He wanted instead to employ museum collections to represent cultures as unique social entities, not simply as steps on a ladder of evolutionary progress. Boas stressed the diversity of American Indian cultures in his displays by dividing up the collections according to culture group. As museological practice developed over the ensuing decades, these ideas proved influential. Clark Wissler, who followed Boas at the American Museum of Natural History, formalized the concept of the more general "culture area" by grouping discrete American Indian cultures organized according to home territory into larger geographic zones: Woodlands, Plains, Southwest, Northwest Coast, and so on. Wissler reasoned that diversity in environment contributed chiefly to diversity in cultural practice.[15] Mason, Boas, and Wissler were all struggling with basic metonymic procedures, the division of collections into component parts by establishing the significance and the logic of the differences between them.

René d'Harnoncourt, director of the Indian Arts and Crafts Board, and Frederic Douglas, an anthropologist and curator of the American Indian collections at the Denver Art Museum, borrowed the metonymic trope of regional and chronological distinctions for their landmark exhibition, *Indian Art of the United States*, which was installed at the Museum of Modern Art in 1941. The exhibition was organized into three large chronological divisions: prehistoric art, living traditions, and Indian art for modern living. The first two sections were then further subdivided into art and culture areas: prehistoric carvers of the far West, carvers of the Northwest Coast, engravers of the Arctic, sculptors of the East, painters, Pueblo corn planters and Navajo shepherds of the Southwest, hunters of the Plains, and woodsmen of the East. The exhibition stressed the metaphor of the objects as art by means of the venue—the Museum of Modern Art—and by strategies of installation that eschewed the natural history display case for clean, white pedestals and platforms with dramatic lighting, the same kind of display strategies employed for the museum's permanent collections.[16]

The metonymic figuration of American Indian culture by "culture area" and by "tribe," together with the allegorical definition of American Indian art, proved to be a durable structuring device for exhibitions. The landmark 1976 exhibition *Sacred Circles* for the Hayward Gallery in London was organized this way, as were Evan Maurer's 1977 exhibition *The Native American Heritage* for the Art Institute of Chicago, the 1972 exhibition *Form and Freedom* at the Walker Art Center in Minneapolis, and, more recently, Canada's 1988 exhibition *The Spirit Sings* at the Glenbow Museum.[17] This figuration is now found in permanent American Indian art museum galleries all across the country. Culture-area divisions may be explained in introductory texts, while the objects are explained by individual labels that may offer information about origin, technique, meaning, or other issues. Rarely is there an attempt to arrange the texts in any kind of sequential narrative that would relate one object to another. The act of choosing the objects for the exhibition signifies their value as art, so it is considered self-evident and requiring no explanation, an appeal to viewers' ability to recognize art when they see it. Modern installation design, like that pioneered at the Museum of Modern Art, tends to reinforce the metaphor of equivalence to European, Asian, or African art. A reflexive, synecdochical counterpart to this kind of exhibition of specific culture areas has also become common, as evidenced in the 1964 exhibition *Yakutat South: Art of the Northwest Coast* at the Art Institute of Chicago, the 1973 exhibition *The Far North* at the National Gallery of Art, and the *Art of the Great Lakes Indian* exhibition held the same year at the Flint Institute of Arts.[18] As the whole is divided into parts, so the parts come to represent the whole through synecdoche.

This kind of "just the facts" installation resembles what White calls an "ideographic" or "formist" mode of historical explanation. To quote White, "The Formist considers an explanation to be complete when a given set of objects has been properly identified, its class, generic, and specific attributes assigned, and labels attesting to its particularity attached to it."[19] A criticism often leveled at this kind of installation is that it has become, over the years, increasingly alienated from the realities of modern Indian interests and experience. In practice, museums have tended to emphasize the past over living culture, to trivialize sacred or religious objects through reclassifying them as simply "painting" or "sculpture," and to neglect living artists. Indian activism over the past few decades eventually forced museums to develop a more critical self-consciousness and involve Indian people who challenged the "self-evident" nature of the representations they found in museums. In 1992, the *Task Force Report on Museums and First Peoples* jointly produced by the Canadian Museums Association and the Assembly of First Nations recommended without equivocation that "museums should ensure that First Peoples are involved in the processes of planning, research implementation, presentation and maintenance of all exhibitions, programs and projects that include Aboriginal cultures."[20]

As a museum governed and staffed by Indian people, the National Museum of the American Indian, as it has developed in the 1990s, is based on this principle. When organizing exhibition representations, however, the problems of figuration still apply. The current NMAI exhibition and catalogue, *Creation's Journey: Masterworks of Native American Identity and Belief,* revives the trope of the metaphorical unity of Native American perspectives, encompassing not only all Native North America, but Meso- and South America as well. To some degree the museum was forced into this position by the range of the collections in its care, the materials assembled under the leadership of George Heye during the first half of this century. While emphasizing the metaphorical unity of Native American perspectives, *Creation's Journey* does not, however, attempt to establish a metaphorical equivalence between Native and European art. On the contrary, the installation texts go to some trouble to reestablish the non-art identities of the objects displayed by describing a great range of culturally rooted meanings for them. These are the "babble of sound, images and politically oriented captions that hopelessly distract from the objects themselves" that Glueck described.[21]

Part of the problem is that the mode of argument is still largely formistic in the sense that each object is discussed separately and, once explained, is not woven into a broader argument beyond being something about American Indians. But to complain about being distracted from the objects is to plead that their now conventional meanings—disembodied things that resemble art in the late-twentieth-century sense of the word, a meaning that is reinforced by the way these objects are housed, mounted, and lit—be allowed to stand unfettered by reconsideration. *New York Times* writer Holland Carter, in his review of the Thaw Collection of American Indian Art at the Fenimore Cooper House, acknowledged that the "passive display" of "objects . . . imbued with spiritual power, inevitably distorts their meaning," but he expressed gratitude that the Cooper House installation kept explanatory texts "to a minimum."[22] In the central hall, the works are only identified by descriptive title, date, material, and tribal origin. Both *Creation's Journey* and the Cooper House installation impose no geographic or chronological ordering on the collections. These exhibitions are instructive complements to one another, as they both emphasize a metaphorical unity of the objects featured, the one verbosely attempting to redefine and recontextualize them, and the other, with the elegance of its visual design, silently reaffirming how most non-Indians have become accustomed to thinking of Indian objects. The one is grounded in situationally transcendent ideology and the other is situationally congruent.

Director W. Richard West of NMAI articulated the central organizing metaphor for *Creation's Journey* when he said in the foreword of the catalogue, "From a Native perspective, objects of material culture are viewed rather differently."[23] This promising statement, of course, begs the question of what the Native perspective is and how it is different. In practice, however, the exhibition demonstrates a plurality of Native perspectives by eliciting interpretive statements from a wide range of participants, both Native and non-Native.[24] Multiple voices of individual testimony have become a familiar device for establishing a Native perspective in exhibition representations. George Horse Capture employed it when, as the organizing curator for the exhibition *Wounded Knee: Lest We Forget*, he could not reconcile contending interpretations of the events offered by different Lakota contingents involved in the planning process. In the end, he allowed each group to write its own labels and declined to offer any additional editorial comment.[25] Multiple voices and multiple curators also characterize all the NMAI exhibitions to date. Some might argue effectively that respect for this kind of personal testimony is rooted in traditional practice. That may be the case, but when privileging this kind of representation one must recognize that the argument will tend to remain rooted in a formist or ideographic mode, subjective and impressionistic in character, which atomizes any potential power of conviction.

The reconciliation of the many Native perspectives with museum practices is not always easy. As Michael Ames once put it, "What happens to museums when their object becomes a speaking subject?"[26] The question poses a classic type of irony, that of paradox. Paradox arises most frequently when the objectives of the museum and those of the collaborative "speaking subject" are not the same, when the ways in which museums and their publics are accustomed to thinking collide with the desires of many Indian people to change that manner of thinking. In some rare instances, individual exhibition projects have been able to exploit this paradox of potentially conflicting objectives as a heuristic device. When Aldona Jonaitis and Gloria Cranmer Webster collaborated on the 1991 American Museum of Natural History exhibition *Chiefly Feasts: The Enduring Kwakiutl Potlatch*, they were faced with the paradox of the museum's desire to display and contextualize

objects collected from the Kwakiutl of British Columbia and the fact that
these objects could only be displayed properly as Kwakiutl family prerogatives and crests during potlatches. The solution was for the museum to
present to its public an exhibition about potlatches, yet there was every indi-
cation that the Kwakiutl involved treated the exhibition itself as a potlatch.
Public events, which offered promotional opportunities from the museum's
point of view, emulated many characteristics of a potlatch. The Kwakiutl
staged their "arrival" on a boat that landed on a westside pier, where they
were greeted by their hosts. During the opening events, a "dance
demonstration" was validated in the Kwakiutl way when Cranmer Webster
distributed "loonies" (Canadian silver dollars) to the assembled guests. The
masks and regalia inside the installation were, in many instances, accompanied by recorded speeches that validated their identities as family posses-
sions. All this created a convincing, educational spectacle for the museum's
audience, but I think the museum missed a beat when it insisted on its
objective standpoint of this event being an exhibition about the potlatch
instead of identifying it as a potlatch. The museum committed thousands of
dollars to exhibition planning and design, so one could argue that its valida-
tion of Kwakiutl family prerogatives was a kind of staged potlatch. The
Kwakiutl participation in various public events reinforces this interpretation,
but unfortunately much of what they did in this context remained unfath-
omable to the New York audience. Perhaps the museum backed off because
it wished to retain its "scientific" objectivity; perhaps the Kwakiutl did not
want to push the analogy of exhibition as potlatch that far. In any case, the
ironies of the project were sublimated in the interest of balance: both parties
got what they wanted, though they were not necessarily the same thing. The
paradox remained veiled to most of the visitors and, one could argue, the
situationally congruent ideologies of the museum remained dominant in
the minds of most of them.[27]

Why is this? Irony, as a trope of figuration, may be misunderstood with
potentially disastrous results. The Royal Ontario Museum attempted to convey an ironic stance toward the African objects collected by Toronto missionaries of the Victorian era, which were displayed in its 1989 exhibition *Into
the Heart of Africa*. The Toronto African-American community failed to see
the ironic attitude of the museum's decision to display and discuss, in this
context, racist literature and illustrations of the period.[28] The installation
attempted the use of antiphrasis, "the ironic trope of negation," in which,
as critic Arnold Krupat put it, "prior assertions are denied in the interest of
promoting opposite or alternative assertions."[29] Evidently, the exhibition did

not adequately deny or disavow the racist content of some of the most offensive display materials, or the African-American community remained blind to their negation. Perhaps the institution, named with all the imperialist resonance of the "Royal Ontario Museum," could not plausibly negate them.

When large public museums employ irony successfully to challenge conventional ways of thinking, there may be other kinds of hell to pay. The general public, by and large, does not expect its museums, particularly the national museums of the Smithsonian Institution, to challenge the central and comforting (for some) myths of national history and identity. William Truetner and the National Museum of American Art discovered this fact when they examined with ironic insight themes of westward expansion and manifest destiny in nineteenth-century American painting in their 1991 exhibition *The West as America*. In retaliation, displeased government representatives attacked Smithsonian funding. With perfect hindsight, this event can be seen as an opening salvo against "leftist leanings" in museums and the arts, to paraphrase Senators Ted Stevens (R-Alaska) and Slade Gorton (R-Wash.), who took the issue to Senate Appropriations Committee hearings in 1991.[30] Sustained attacks have crippled the National Endowment for the Arts and National Endowment for the Humanities. More recently, National Air and Space Museum director Martin Harwit lost his job over disagreements about how the atomic bombing of Japan should be interpreted in an exhibition on the Enola Gay, the B-29 bomber that dropped the atomic bomb on Hiroshima near the end of World War II. The facts in dispute revolved around the number of U.S. lives saved as a result of dropping the bomb (a hypothetical number, at best) and the degree to which representations of the event should sympathetically treat the suffering of Japanese people. When John Correll, editor of *AIR FORCE Magazine* and one of the chief antagonists, wrote that people were "not interested in counterculture morality pageants put on by academic activists," he acknowledged that he was battling over contending ideologies, not facts.[31]

The issue of who is speaking is central to irony. Irony has been employed more successfully by Indian artists and curators to challenge conventional thought, but in venues that are not vested with the public authority of the Smithsonian. *Fluffs and Feathers*, organized by Tom Hill for the Woodland Indian Cultural Centre in Brantford, Ontario, examined Indian stereotypes through the display of Indian kitsch.[32] Gerald McMaster's *Savage Graces* presented the artist's powerful examination of the same subject in small museums throughout Canada.[33] Both exhibitions were far more successful in positioning themselves ironically between their object and their audience, but both failed to draw the kind of public and press attention that would change habitual ways of thinking.

What is really at stake? The historical and ethical relations between Native Americans and Euro-Americans, I would argue, remain the most central, underlying problem of American identity. The uneasiness and weight of this question in the public mind is made obvious in the popular media, which, because of their market orientation, have a much firmer grip on the American pulse than museums do. The success of *Dances with Wolves* among non-Indian Americans stemmed, I think, from a feeling of giddy relief. Ainsley Dunbar (Kevin Costner), representing an ethnically and environmentally sensitive citizen of the 1990s, traveled back in time and reassured moviegoers that, if they had known then what they know now, the nineteenth-century Lakota would have liked them too.

America does not know how to think or talk about Indians. As Arnold Krupat notes in his book *Ethnocriticism*, the American myth traps American Indians in a kind of pendulum course that veers back and forth between the classical emplotments of comedy and tragedy. As in a comedy, the Indian poses a temporary obstacle to be overcome by American society in its progress toward the reconciliation of all as "civilization." If this myth seems too cheerfully oblivious to the sufferings of Indian people, the same story can be cast as a tragedy, the sad yet inevitable fate of Indians in the face of progress.[34] No small wonder that Indian people themselves feel left out of either story. In fact, both emplotments of American history leave Indians in the past as opponents who were overcome or as the remnant of some bygone time. Universally, in my experience, Indian people now demand that they be restored to the American story, not as ingredients in the melting pot or as fossils, but as sovereignties who have suffered at the hands of European conquerors but who have survived. This is a romantic emplotment, the narrative of a spiritual quest for salvation made difficult with struggle. White wrote, "The Romance is fundamentally a drama of self-identification symbolized by the hero's transcendence of the world of experience, his victory over it, and his final liberation from it. . . . It is a drama of the triumph of good over evil, of virtue over vice, of light over darkness, and of the ultimate transcendence of man over the world in which he was imprisoned."[35] The survival of American Indian culture to the present day, despite every effort to destroy it, is such a transcendence. As photographer and critic Theresa Harlan put it, "Native survival was and remains a contest over life, humanity, land, systems of knowledge, memory, and representations."[36] In my experience, this singular idea is emphasized with insistence—

every representation of Indian people in museums should include proof of survival.

Literary criticism identifies four archetypical kinds of stories: comedy, tragedy, romance, and ironic satire. White has shown that these same kinds of archetypical emplotments apply to historical narratives, the ways in which history is told to make sense of otherwise incomprehensible sequences of events. It seems to me that when non-Native Americans consider their nation's history in relation to Indians, they tend to tell stories of comedy and tragedy. When Native American people have reflected on the history of their experiences with non-Natives, they often speak in terms of irony and romantic transcendence. Are there other ways to structure narratives from a Native American perspective? I am not qualified to say, though I sense that Indian curators and artists are struggling to find them.

Exhibitions, however, are cultural events beyond the power of any single individual, or group of individuals, to shape and control them. When I was organizing the 1992 exhibition *Art of the American Indian Frontier: The Collecting of Chandler and Pohrt* for an opening at the National Gallery of Art in Washington, D.C., I was less cognizant of the foregoing issues than I am now, but I was certainly aware that there was a lot at stake. The exhibition featured 150 objects produced by more than twenty different Woodland and Plains peoples. The objects, selected from a group of over four thousand items dispersed among several museums, had been collected by Milford Chandler and Richard Pohrt between 1915 and 1990—a remarkable achievement, the recognition of which was the underlying purpose of the exhibition. With the help of George Horse Capture as co-curator, the advice of Dave Warren, Nancy Lurie, and Joe Porter as a working committee, and funding from the National Endowment for the Humanities, we developed a simple core narrative for the show: art as a strategy of survival. Horse Capture proposed including works by living artists, but the Chandler-Pohrt collection had none, and Richard Pohrt, who was part of the planning team, was against it. So the exhibition included objects dating no earlier than about 1780 and no later than perhaps 1920. This period of American Indian history is frequently depicted as an episode of cultural decline. On the other hand, craft and visual-arts traditions flourished during this time with the invention, development, and elaboration of glass-bead embroidery, woven beadwork, ribbon work, and remarkable developments in the traditions of pictographic arts, wood and stone carving, and visionary painting on traditional objects. These arts, we concluded, grew as a means of asserting cultural identity at a time when cultural survival was increasingly threatened by the outside world. These ideas were addressed in gallery texts, case texts, and individual object labels, as well as in an audio tour written and narrated by Horse Capture and me, and in the catalogue.[37] We decided to deal with the sources of the collection separately, in a short film about Chandler and Pohrt that would serve as an adjunct to the exhibition and not conflict with its central theme.[38] A symposium co-organized with NMAI focused on the multiple, and often subjective and personal, meanings of objects.[39] Similar symposia were organized at the other participating venues: the Seattle Art Museum, the Dallas Museum of Art, the Buffalo Bill Historical Center, and the Detroit Institute of Arts.

Despite our interests in contextualizing the objects, the National Gallery, by virtue of the very nature of the institution, stressed the metaphorical equivalence between the objects in the show and anything else they installed there. As the nation's premier art gallery, expressing the humanistic unity of all the world's art is their stock in trade. The designers applied themselves to the Chandler-Pohrt exhibition with the same energy and vision they had shown when designing *The English Country House* exhibition. The Chandler-Pohrt show was accompanied at various times by exhibitions of John Singer Sargent, Kathe Kollwitz, and Hellenistic Greek bronzes.[40] We felt the prominence of the National Gallery as a venue was worth it and, in some ways, we enjoyed the ironies. As Horse Capture put it in a *Washington Post* interview, "We are proud of this national recognition that our art *is* art, but all these things were made to be used, not hung on a wall." Hank Burchard, the reporter, accepted this paradoxical statement as evidence of the "inherent dilemma in showing Indian artifacts."[41] For Jed Perl, critic for *The New Criterion*, the metaphor did not stand up. He complained that many of the objects in the show were not "significant works of art," chided the National Gallery for a "cold and sterile" installation, and "felt nostalgic for the old ethnographic presentations."[42] *The Art Newspaper* quoted my essay in the catalogue, in which I said it "is not so much an issue of defining American Indian creations to fit a European definition of art, but of redefining art to include the artistic practices of American Indians."[43] *Washington Times* critic Eric Gibson seemed to get it; his headline read, "Captivating Indian Show Tells Intent Behind Items."[44] But I think we all understood the conflict between the National Gallery installation and the ideological aspirations of the project. Like most exhibition projects, it was a balancing act.

I was reminded that the conflict is real and sometimes heated when the show arrived in Detroit. Despite support from the Michigan Commission of Indian Affairs and virtually the entire leadership of the Detroit and Michigan Native communities, a small group of young Native Americans decided to protest the exhibition. A statement in their press release put a finger on the problem: "There is a difference between what is art and what is sacred. . . . You cannot promote and desecrate at the same time."[45] As it turned out, they had no specific complaint about any single object or group of objects. They reasoned that everything in the show represented a sacred cultural patrimony. Conversations with provisionally supportive Native visitors to the show brought the point home to me. Hap McQue, a teacher of the Ojibwe language, responded to my query about how he liked the show by saying, "It makes me sad." It was my impression through conversations like these that many Native visitors to the galleries could not look at the collections without being reminded of what they had lost. Some supported the museum's efforts to approximate some kind of recovery. "How are people going to know how Native Americans dressed and survived in those days?" said Edith Young, a Tlingit educator.[46] Others, like the protesters, simply could not proceed beyond their anger.

The need to change the way Native Americans are represented in museums, films, and literature cannot be addressed by any one project. As they are, representations are simply reflections of attitudes, habitual ways of thinking that are not easily changed. We should not be surprised at resistance when we challenge those attitudes with different representations, and we should learn to expect corrective measures from the press, our governing bodies, and our public when we do so.

NOTES

1. Hayden White, *Tropics of Discourse: Essays in Cultural Criticism* (Baltimore: Johns Hopkins University Press, 1978), 1.

2. The sessions were sponsored in part by the Texas Commission for the Arts and consisted of round-table discussions from 5 to 7 November 1992. Participants included Richard Bretell, Emily Sano, and Carol Robbins from the Dallas Museum of Art, and Linda L. Vann, Virgil H. Swift, Voce Durling-Jones, Annia Silas, Mary Helen Deer Smith, Alan Govenar, and David Alcoze from the advisory group.

3. Timothy W. Luke, *Shows of Force: Power, Politics, and Ideology in Art Exhibitions* (Durham: Duke University Press, 1992), 1.

4. Karl Mannheim, "Conservative Thought," *Essays on Sociology and Social Psychology*, ed. Paul Kecskemeti (New York: Oxford University Press, 1953). Hayden White applied

Mannheim's ideas to his interpretation of ideology in White, *Tropics of Discourse*, 68–69.

5. Amy Gamerman, "Indian Art Takes Shelter in Beaux-Arts Wickiup," *Wall Street Journal*, 17 November 1992, sec. A, p. 16; and Grace Glueck, "Ethnic Culture and Slick Theatrics: Mural and Method," *New York Times*, 16 January 1995.

6. James Clifford, "On Ethnographic Allegory," in *Writing Culture: The Poetics and Politics of Ethnography*, ed. James Clifford and George E. Marcus (Berkeley: University of California Press, 1986), 98–121.

7. The ethnocentric bias of these terms as they have been employed in anthropology is discussed briefly in Wyatt MacGaffey, *Religion and Society in Central Africa: The BaKongo of Lower Zaire* (Chicago: University of Chicago Press, 1986), 2–3.

8. My knowledge of these enterprises comes from correspondence between Dolly Sloan and Amelia Elizabeth White in the Amelia Elizabeth White papers at the School for American Research in Santa Fe, N. Mex.

9. Frederick Webb Hodge, Herbert J. Spinden, and Oliver LaFarge, *Introduction to American Indian Art*, 2 vols. (New York: Exposition of Indian Tribal Arts, 1931; reprint, 2 vols. in 1, Glorieta, N. Mex.: Rio Grande Press), 1:15.

10. Kenneth Burke, *A Grammar of Motives* (Berkeley: University of California Press, 1969), 503–17. Hayden White applied Burke's definitions of "master tropes" in his discussion in White, *Tropics of Discourse*, 1–25.

11. Hodge, Spinden, and LaFarge, *Introduction to American Indian Art*, 1:13.

12. Ibid., 1:59.

13. Ibid., 2d vol.

14. See Samuel E. Watson III, "Stylistic Plurality in the Paintings of Albert Looking Elk: An Examination of Patronage," in *American Indian Art Magazine* 20 (Winter 1994): 62–69; and W. Jackson Rushing, "Authenticity and Subjectivity in Post-War Painting: Concerning Herrera, Scholder, and Cannon," *Shared Visions: Native American Painters and Sculptors in the Twentieth Century*, 2d ed., ed. Margaret Archuleta and Rennard Strickland (New York: New Press, 1991), 12–21.

15. For a discussion of the Boas and Mason controversy, see Aldona Jonaitis, *From the Land of the Totem Poles: The Northwest Coast Indian Art Collection at the American Museum of Natural History* (New York: American Museum of Natural History; Seattle: University of Washington Press, 1988), 126–28, 217–18.

16. See René d'Harnoncourt and Frederic Douglas, *Indian Art of the United States* (New York: Museum of Modern Art, 1941); W. Jackson Rushing, "Marketing the Affinity of the Primitive and the Modern: René d'Harnoncourt and 'Indian Art of the United States,'" in *The Early Years of Native American Art History: The Politics of Scholarship and Collecting*, ed. Janet Catherine Berlo (Seattle: University of Washington Press; Vancouver: University of British Columbia Press, 1992), 191–236; and Robert Fay Schrader, *The Indian Arts and Crafts Board: An Aspect of New Deal Indian Policy* (Albuquerque: University of New Mexico Press, 1983), 223–41.

17. Ralph T. Coe, *Sacred Circles: Two Thousand Years of North American Indian Art* (London: Arts Council of Great Britain, 1976); Evan M. Maurer, *The Native American Heritage: A Survey of North American Indian Art* (Chicago: Art Institute of Chicago, 1977); Mildred Friedman, Dean Swanson, and David Ryan, eds., *American Indian Art: Form and Tradition* (Minneapolis: Walker Art Center and the Minneapolis Institute of Arts, 1972); and Glenbow Museum, *The Spirit Sings: Artistic Traditions of Canada's First Peoples* (Toronto: McClelland and Stewart in association with Glenbow Museum, 1987).

18. Allen Wardwell, *Yakutat South: Indian Art of the Northwest Coast* (Chicago: Art Institute of Chicago, 1964); Henry B. Collins et al., *The Far North: Two Thousand Years of American Eskimo and Indian Art* (Washington, D.C.: National Gallery of Art, 1973); and Flint Institute of Arts, *The Art of the Great Lakes Indians* (Flint, Mich.: Flint Institute of Arts, 1973).

19. Hayden White, *Metahistory: The Historical Imagination in Nineteenth-Century Europe* (Baltimore: Johns Hopkins University Press, 1973), 14; see also White, *Tropics of Discourse*, 64–65.

20. *Turning the Page: Forging New Partnerships between Museums and First Peoples* (Ottawa: Assembly of First Nations, Canadian Museums Association, 1992).

21. Glueck, "Ethnic Culture and Slick Theatrics."

22. Holland Carter, "Indelible Visions of a Faded World," *New York Times*, 23 July 1995, final late edition, sec. 2, p. 35, col. 1. Interestingly enough, a small publication that accompanied the opening of the Eugene and Clare Thaw Wing is organized by culture area; see Gilbert T. Vincent, *Masterpieces of American Indian Art from the Eugene and Clare Thaw Collection* (New York: Harry W. Abrams, Inc., in association with the New York State Historical Association, 1995).

23. W. Richard West, Jr., "Foreword," *Creation's Journey: Native American Identity and Belief*, ed. Tom Hill and Richard W. Hill, Sr. (Washington, D.C.: Smithsonian Institution Press in association with the National Museum of the American Indian, 1994), 10.

24. Many of the interpretive texts were written by the staff at the National Museum of the American Indian. Other statements are quoted from the writings of Alfred Young Man, Robert Houle, Ruth Bunzel, Claude Levi-Strauss, Frank Hamilton Cushing, Deborah Doxtator, and many others.

25. See George P. Horse Capture, introduction to *Wounded Knee: Lest We Forget*, by Alvin M. Josephy, Jr., Trudy Thomas, and Jeanne Eder (Cody, Wyo.: Buffalo Bill Historical Center, 1990). The exhibition was organized by the Buffalo Bill Historical Center, and was presented 17 September to 30 November 1990. I learned of Horse Capture's difficulties with the interpretive texts for the exhibition through personal communication with him.

26. Michael M. Ames, "What Happens When the Object Becomes the Subject?" *Harbour Magazine of Everyday Life* 3 (Winter 1993–94): 63–65.

27. *Chiefly Feasts: The Enduring Kwakiutl Potlatch*, an exhibition organized by Aldona Jonaitis for the American Museum of Natural History, was presented October 1991 to February 1992. I attended many of the opening events, and my interpretations of

them stem from several conversations with Jonaitis and Gloria Cranmer Webster on various occasions. I developed some of these ideas in "Letter from the President," *Native American Art Studies Association Newsletter*, 8 (Summer 1992).

28. See Simon Ottenburg, "Into the Heart of Africa," *African Arts* 24 (July 1991): 79–82.

29. Arnold Krupat, *Ethnocriticism: Ethnography, History, Literature* (Berkeley: University of California Press, 1992), 86–87.

30. See Michael Kimmelman, "Old West, New Twist at the Smithsonian," *New York Times,* 26 May 1991, late final edition, sec. 2, p. 1, col. 1.

31. See Mike Wallace, "The Battle of the Enola Gay," *Museum News* 74 (July/August 1995): 40–45, 60–62.

32. See Deborah Doxtator, *Fluffs and Feathers: A Resource Guide* (Brantford, Ont.: Woodland Indian Cultural Centre, 1988).

33. See *Savage Graces*: "After Images," *Harbour Magazine of Everyday Life* (Winter 1993–94). The issue was produced in collaboration with the University of British Columbia Museum of Anthropology for the exhibition, *Savage Graces,* which opened at University of British Columbia on 28 July 1992. I saw the exhibition at the Windsor Art Gallery (Windsor, Ontario) where it was shown 17 September to 12 November 1994.

34. Krupat, *Ethnocriticism,* 132–36.

35. White, *Metahistory,* 8–9.

36. Theresa Harlan, "Creating a Visual History: A Question of Ownership," *Aperture* (Summer 1995): 20.

37. See David W. Penney, *Art of the American Indian Frontier: The Chandler-Pohrt Collection* (Seattle: University of Washington Press, 1992).

38. *The Journey of the Chandler-Pohrt Collection.* Videocassette produced by Pamela Conn and Sue Marx. 17 min. The Detroit Institute of Arts, 1992.

39. The symposium, *Perspectives on American Indian Art,* was held at the National Gallery of Art, Washington, D.C., 3 October 1992.

40. *Art of the American Indian Frontier: The Collecting of Chandler and Pohrt* was on exhibit 24 May 1992 to 24 January 1993 at the National Gallery of Art, Washington, D.C.

41. Hank Burchard, "Native Arts, Tribal Spirits," *Washington Post,* 22 May 1992.

42. Jed Perl, "Curators and Indians," *The New Criterion,* 2 (October 1992): 53–56.

43. James Edward Kaufman, "National Gallery Brings American Indians into the Tribe of the New Art History," *The Art Newspaper* (June 1992).

44. Eric Gibson, "Captivating Indian Show Tells Intent Behind Items," *Washington Times,* 24 May 1992.

45. The press release was distributed by fax beginning 24 March 1992.

46. Edith Young was quoted in Cecil Angel, "DIA Exhibit of Indian Frontier Artifacts Draws Protest," *Detroit Free Press*, 26 March 1994.

The Integration of Traditional Indian Beliefs into the Museum at Warm Springs

JANICE CLEMENTS

The Museum at Warm Springs, located on the Confederated Tribes of the Warm Springs Reservation in Oregon, opened in March 1993 and represents a special history in several ways. Three tribes—the Sahaptin-speaking Warm Springs Tribe, the Upper Chinook–speaking Wascos, and the Northern Paiute—have shared this Northwest territory for eight thousand years, and the reservation since its establishment with the Treaty of 1855. The artifacts and other presentations in the new museum, including the building's novel architecture, attest to a cultural continuity spanning centuries. In traditional Native American cultures, art was not a separate pursuit, and the Warm Springs museum exhibition shows how beauty and utility uniquely combined in objects of everyday use to reflect a way of life and an aesthetic that respected the interrelationship between Earth and its inhabitants. The museum is a conservatory for the ancient and honored traditions of the thirty-five hundred Confederated Tribal members living on the reservation. It is also an invitation to the public to understand another dimension of American culture.

The history of the museum is also special. In 1968, tribal leaders began setting aside $50,000 every year for the purchase of Native artifacts—family heirlooms, items obtained from other tribes, and gifts and keepsakes—from families in the Warm Springs region. The museum also collected twenty-five hundred photographs dating back to the 1850s, important tribal documents, and books on Indian history, art, and culture. This collection initiative began in response to outside dealers and institutions buying up Native material culture. We needed to preserve a piece of our heritage for future generations.

Since 1968, we have spent nearly one million dollars acquiring these cultural heirlooms, making the Warm Springs museum one of the most complete Native American collections owned by an Indian tribe. Our efforts also represent the most aggressive acquisitions program ever undertaken

Fig. 9. The Museum at Warm Springs. Photo by Beth Russell.

by an American Indian group. We can look upon our success as the product of community support and commitment.

After twenty years of collecting these artifacts, the tribal council members made building the museum their top priority. They were concerned about the future of our young people, and believed the museum could educate them about their heritage and instill cultural values. Thus, the museum was really built for our children, and bears this dedication to them: "To our children, those of this lifetime and those of many generations to follow, we leave this legacy: preservation of the past, the birthright of your heritage; and the inheritance of our hopes and dreams for the future." Above the entrance to the museum is a word from the Sahaptin language, *twanat*, which means "I will follow for generations to come." Our young people can go to the museum, learn about themselves, and follow in the ways of their people.

Community members became more committed to the museum when they realized that our mission was to help preserve and strengthen our cultural traditions. In October 1988, tribal members appropriated $2.5 million for a building, but our struggle had only begun. We needed a museum director and millions more in funding to construct the building, which we were able to raise through the help of foundations, corporations, and private donors. In all, the Confederated Tribes contributed over three million dollars, the largest sum ever allocated for the building of a museum by a Native American tribe. An additional $3.1 million came from outside sources.

The Museum at Warm Springs is the first tribal museum in the state of Oregon. The building is a monument to the three tribal cultures living together on the Warm Springs Reservation. Its design evokes a traditional

Fig. 10. Klickitat basket. Courtesy of the Museum at Warm Springs.

desert encampment set among cottonwoods next to the Shitike Creek. The roof lines of a tule-mat lodge, a curved ceiling plankhouse, and a wick-iup (reed hut) represent the Warm Springs, the Wasco, and the Paiute tribes (fig. 9).

Historically, the Warm Springs and Paiute were semi-nomadic and nomadic hunters and gatherers, and the Wasco were fishermen and traders. The museum reflects the tribes' harmony with the natural environment. The building's creative use of natural stone, heavy timber, and brick demonstrates our tradition of incorporating art into everyday life. Tribal symbols such as the drum and Klickitat basket patterns (fig. 10) also appear in the museum's architectural design. The front door's steel handles have their origins in the Indian dance bustle.

Visitors arrive at a reflective pool and follow a stream to a circular stone drum, which is the museum entrance. To Indians, the drum symbolizes the heartbeat of all living things. The building was designed by Portland architects Donald Stastny and Bryan Burke, who invited tribal members to participate in the planning by sharing their stories, dreams, and ideas. Stastny has said, "The Indians guided us along a spiritual path toward the right solution." Native spirituality has played a continuous role in the museum's development, as it does in the daily life of the reservation community.

The museum's permanent, interactive exhibition shows a video called *Songs of Our People*, in which members from the three tribes sing and drum traditional songs. In another short film, *According to the Earth*, tribal elders

Fig. 11. Diorama depicting a Wasco wedding. Photo by Olney Patt, Jr.

speak about the importance of preserving Native languages and traditions, and about their hardship during the early years of reservation life. Viewers also learn about the "legal land grab" caused by the 1887 Dawes Act, which was successfully resisted by the Confederated Tribes. All told, the museum devotes considerable space to tribal history.

The permanent collection also features reproductions of traditional dwellings, an extensive collection of storage containers, including Klickitat baskets, Wasco Sally bags, Warm Springs cornhusk bags, and a diorama depicting a Wasco wedding (fig. 11). In this replica of a cultural tradition, tribal families trade abundant supplies of food, clothing, jewelry, a horse, and the like. In another location, visitors are invited to learn simple phrases in the Sahaptin, Chinookian, and Wasco dialects. These are a small sampling of our materials and themes.

The museum also features a changing exhibition gallery, a library and archives, a conservation lab, and classrooms for workshops and living-history demonstrations. As visitors leave the permanent exhibition, large photographic cutouts of reservation residents bid them farewell, affirming a message of "respect for fellow humans and for Mother Earth as the foundations of achievement and the roots of true progress."

Four tribal members and three non-Natives make up the museum's board of directors. This has been a positive combination because the non-

Native members help steer discussion back on course when tribal politics threaten business proceedings. Chief Delvis Heath, Sr., is president of the board. Our museum staff of twelve handles everything from development to running the gift shop.

Our twenty-five-thousand-square-foot museum continues to grow and evolve. We now have tribal members scheduled to engage in some kind of cultural activity every weekend during the spring and summer. Our volume of visitors assures future construction of galleries and exhibition projects, including a children's museum and an outdoor "natural environment" exhibition. We will use the Shitike Creek to show how water, the source of all life, is vital and integral to our culture. At twice-yearly food celebrations, we line up our foods and the water and sing about them. Our young people, who are unfamiliar with these religious songs, can now learn about them in the museum. If our youth truly believe in our ways as Native Americans, they can gain more wisdom from their own cultural heritage than from outside sources telling them how to live their lives.

When I went to boarding school, we learned about the cowboys and the Indians and how the white people were the good people. We yelled for the cavalry when it came time to kill the Indians. This was how we thought in the 1940s, but today we realize the wealth and value of our history. Many people come to the Museum at Warm Springs to learn how it was started because they want to build a museum for themselves and for their future.

Are Changing Representations of First Peoples in Canadian Museums and Galleries Challenging the Curatorial Prerogative?

MICHAEL M. AMES

Collaboration between curators and First Peoples who are represented in exhibitions has become a standard for art and anthropology exhibitions in Canadian museums and galleries (fig. 12), though the interaction is not without controversy. The new dynamic raises a significant question: How does this collaboration challenge the traditional curatorial prerogative and affect the quality of the works displayed? An examination of recent initiatives suggests that these new representational strategies alter the powers and responsibilities of curators, and influence what is selected for exhibition. In January 1992, the Assembly of First Nations (AFN) and the Canadian Museums Association (CMA) issued the joint *Task Force Report on Museums and First Peoples,* which represented two years of discussion between members of the First Nations and museum communities.[1] This report stated that it was "necessary to develop new relationships with museums based on progressive principles and policy."[2] Museums across Canada promptly agreed that the recommendations were guidelines for future action. Museum representatives talked about a new, more positive era in relations between First Peoples and museums.

Has progress been made since this report was issued and proclaimed as a new standard for Canadian museums? Have museums implemented changes in the representation of First Peoples in response to the recommendations? Despite the Task Force's recommendation that a joint First Peoples–museum committee be formed "to monitor and report developments over a five year period," no national survey has been conducted, though a report is being prepared by Trudy Nicks, co-author of the Task Force report.[3] Because of this lack of data, I can only give my impressions, drawn from my own experience at the Museum of Anthropology at the University of British Columbia. It would be reasonable to say that the report represented an important step forward in articulating a constructive set of principles for Canadian museums, and that some positive developments

Fig. 12. Musqueam Elders Dominic Point and Vincent Stogan lead the Coast Salish participants and other delegates to the opening of *World Conference: Indigenous Peoples Education,*
1987. Courtesy of the University of British Columbia Museum of Anthropology.

have occurred. It is also my impression that these developments fall considerably short of expectations, since policies are always easier to espouse than
to put into practice. There may also be valid reasons why changes appear to
be gradual.

The Task Force recommendations were based on the fundamental principle that First Peoples own or have moral claim to their heritage and therefore should participate equally in its preservation and presentation. Several
Task Force recommendations illustrate this principle:

1. Museums and First Peoples will work together to correct
   inequities that have characterized their relationships in the past.
2. First Peoples and museums must accept the philosophy of co-
   management and co-responsibility.
3. Appropriate representatives of First Peoples will be involved as
   equal partners in any museum exhibition, program, or project
   dealing with Aboriginal heritage, history, or culture.
4. First Peoples must be fully involved in the development of policies and funding programs related to Aboriginal heritage, history, and culture.[4]

The emphasis of the Task Force recommendations was on equality of relationships between museums and First Nations, entailing an equality of
power and responsibility (fig. 13). Equality is a difficult principle to define,
let alone to implement, especially when the parties to a relationship hold

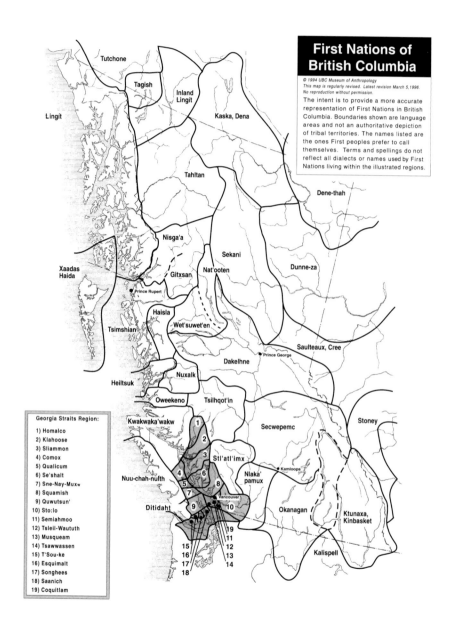

Fig. 13. First Nations map. An example of collaboration with First Nations is the map of their territories listing the names First Nations use themselves rather than names ascribed to them by others. The British Columbia map was prepared under the supervision of Pam Brown, Curator of Ethnology/Media, Museum of Anthropology. Courtesy of the University of British Columbia Museum of Anthropology.

different interests and priorities. So far the definitions for equality have begun from an institutional perspective: the museum's mandate, schedule, funding level, and audience, as well as the curator's experience and interest. Thus, an inequality is built into the relationship from the outset, so that achieving a balance in relationships becomes a struggle regardless of official museum rhetoric.

It has been suggested that the Task Force recommendations actually perpetuate a structural imbalance. In her searching criticism of the *Task Force Report*, Deborah Doxtator wrote:

> [I]ts recommendations generally ascribe most of the responsibilities . . . to non-Native museums who must, out of moral compunction, "involve" Aboriginal people by allowing them access to the museum's collections. Aboriginal peoples are given a somewhat passive role in these recommendations. . . . Since non-Native museums administer most of the material heritage of Aboriginal peoples and the Canadian government controls the funding of Aboriginal cultural programs, the goals of Euro-Canadian society for intellectual stimulation and cultural growth have been met to a far greater degree than have the needs of Aboriginal communities for a sense of self-knowing, self-worth, and self-determination.[5]

I suspect that if a careful examination were made of Canadian museum responses to the Task Force recommendations, Doxtator's criticisms would find considerable support. Nevertheless, at least three developments are influencing the presentation of Aboriginal art and heritage: (1) the employment of First Peoples by museums, (2) increased effort to collaborate, and (3) more opportunities for Aboriginal curators to mount their own exhibitions.[6] These are positive initiatives, and no doubt some museums are trying to do even more. The question is, how are these initiatives being put into practice?

The Appointment of Aboriginal People to Museums

A number of museums have made concentrated efforts to add First Peoples to their permanent staffs, but so far the effort has been minimal. First, few positions are available during the present era of declining budgets. Second, it will take years before new appointees reach senior levels—if they bother to stay that long. Third, it exposes candidates in minority positions to allegations of tokenism. Finally, it is difficult to find Aboriginal people who are both interested and qualified to work in museums. Those who do accept

Fig. 14. Margaret Ann Harris of the Dag'm Haast Dancers in the production of "Gawa Gyani," 1991. Courtesy of the University of British Columbia Museum of Anthropology.

museum employment are subject to criticism by other Aboriginal people, because museums as we know them are essentially white European inventions designed to serve the interests of mainstream or non-Aboriginal segments of society. As art historian Carol Duncan has observed, a museum is an "ideologically active environment," and the value of that environment is not self-evident to most First Peoples, nor is the museum's internal organizational culture entirely compatible with Aboriginal sentiments.[7] Even so, it is likely that the few Aboriginal people who are employed in Canadian museums are introducing changes in the representation of First Nations.

Collaboration between First Peoples and Museums

There are at least two forms of collaboration between First Peoples and museums: (1) museums recruit First Peoples as consultants, advisors, or as artists whose works are to be exhibited; and (2) museums engage in more fundamental partnerships with First Peoples, partnerships that recognize joint custody of the collections and collaboration in collections management, storage, and exhibition. The first way of collaboration is more common, perhaps because it is easier and more profitable for museums. The second way—sharing authority over the collections—occurs less often and has greater impact on museums.

(1) *First Peoples as Resource.* An example of the first type of collaboration can be found in the production of an Aboriginal art or history exhibition. Typically, the relationship would be between a museum's curatorial team and the artists and Aboriginal resource people—the elders, cultural experts, or performers (fig. 14). In this situation, the traditional curatorial prerogative usually prevails because of academic training, connoisseurship built on years of experience, and control over the exhibition schedule and budget.

This curatorial prerogative may be different in art galleries and art museums than in anthropology museums. Most art curators are trained in Western art history, which derives its doctrines from the world's centers of Western art, such as Paris, London, and New York. Institutions like New York's Museum of Modern Art and Metropolitan Museum of Art provide standard North American interpretations of this Western art-history perspective. The National Gallery of Canada, the Montreal Museum of Fine Arts, and the Art Gallery of Ontario are major Canadian institutions also working within this Western-world perspective. Fine art and good artists, according to this view, transcend society, work independently of and often in opposition to it, and challenge the present by experimenting with the new or the avant-garde.[8] For reference purposes, this view can be characterized as the "transcendental perspective." Since art transcends normal conventions, curators assume a position that transcends even the artists, because of their more extensive knowledge of that transcendence.

Curators working within the traditions of the "new art history" or anthropology tend to temper this transcendental model with a form of ethnographic relativism, which allows art to be identified separately from other aspects of culture and seen within its cultural and historical context.[9] We might call this a Western "contextualized perspective." Accordingly, anthropological curators allow their expertise to be contextually informed. The need to obtain contextual information naturally opens the door to collaboration with artists and other cultural experts who may exert some influence on the resulting exhibition. The ground rules for collaboration, however, remain those of the institution, since the contextual curator still makes the final decisions regarding what is to be included and how it is to be interpreted. The curator also typically writes the introductory essay for the accompanying catalogue, thereby framing the whole project.

The different ways in which transcendental and contextual approaches define the curatorial prerogative were illustrated during the 1994 exhibition of Inuit art at the Canadian Museum of Civilization in Hull, Quebec. It was, according to a newspaper report, a "curatorial square-off" over who should exercise the final authority: a professional curator who knows better than the artists, or a curator who consults with them?[10]

According to comments in the exhibition catalogue by Inuit specialist and Carleton University art historian Marion Jackson, the Canadian Museum of Civilization rejected the curatorial tradition of interpreting Aboriginal art in terms of academic criteria in favor of involving the artists themselves in the interpretation of their own works. Exhibition curator Odette Leroux conducted lengthy interviews with the artists, which was reportedly the first time some of them had been asked to record their own opinions of their work. Leroux used these interviews to select pieces for the exhibitions, choosing works on which the artists had commented.

Norman Zepp, a former curator of Inuit art at the Art Gallery of Ontario, disagreed with this procedure. He held that allowing artists to participate in the selection of works was a retreat from scholarship. Artists are not, according to Zepp, the best judges of their own work; that is the curator's responsibility. "If I am critical of some of the work," he said (and he was), "it's because I know how great Inuit art can be." Leroux's approach, Zepp said, has "overtones of ethnography" and "romanticizes and holds back the art."[11] (Presumably art historians do not romanticize when they use the Western art tradition as a universal standard.)

From Leroux's standpoint, the curator cannot understand the aesthetics without discussing the ethnography, the artists' social experiences, and the cultural settings. Leroux said that the final decision about what works were shown was hers. Her error, according to the transcendental-curator-as-final-authority perspective, was allowing the artists to influence her judgments. Traditional curators see this as a submission to political correctness, whereas anthropologically oriented curators see it as a necessary recognition of cultural context.

Exhibitions produced by Aboriginal curators generally have avoided these academic arguments in favor of a more holistic perspective. Before examining the Aboriginal prerogative, however, I want to consider an example of the second kind of collaboration between museums and First Peoples.

(2) *First Peoples as Full Partners.* Accepting First Peoples as full partners in a project has more radical implications for a museum than treating them as sources of art or contextual information. A full-partner relationship entails a more equitable balance in power and responsibilities and, at the least, introduces outside partners, creating a relationship that is more difficult for an institution to control.

Examples of this are two archaeological exhibitions prepared at the University of British Columbia's Museum of Anthropology in 1995 and 1996, *From Under the Delta: Wet-site Archaeology in the Lower Fraser Delta* and *Written in the Earth.* Both involve pre-Contact materials excavated from the Greater Vancouver region. These rare items are two to four thousand years old, and many are fragile. Each exhibition was initiated by an archaeological curator, supported by a team of other archaeologists, a designer, and a conservation technician. The aesthetic qualities of the objects were to be featured along with archaeological interpretations.

While preparing exhibition-grant applications, the two teams, in keeping with Task Force recommendations, sought consent from those band councils whose heritage was to be exhibited. The councils gave their consent on the condition that their representatives be consulted on the selection and interpretation of materials. The Musqueam Band took a greater interest in the proceedings, since most of the artifacts came from their traditional territories and the Museum of Anthropology stands on their traditional land. The Musqueam Council's consent differed in that it would be renegotiated at each stage of the exhibition, from preparation to the return of materials to museum storage at the conclusion of the two exhibitions. The Council reserved the right to withdraw approval for either exhibition at any point should the museum fail to meet the standards of performance agreed to during the consultation process. Withdrawal of approval would shut down the exhibition because the museum would be obliged to withdraw Musqueam objects. These procedures were agreed upon by both the Band Council and the museum. The concept of collaboration quickly took on a new meaning for the two exhibition teams and the museum. Traditional roles were practically reversed, with museum staff becoming the consultants or resource people, and the Band Council becoming the partner with final authority.

From Under the Delta opened in April 1996 and *Written in the Earth* in October 1996, both with approval of the participating bands. We learned from these exhibitions that the process is as important as the outcome, although it was not always an easy process for the museum to accommodate. Four observations are worth noting.

First, the museum was asked to recognize that moral ownership of the collections resides with First Nations, even where a legal title may be held by the government or a lending museum. This was not a difficult principle to accept. Most of the objects selected for exhibition were excavated under provincial government permit and therefore are legally held "in trust" by museums at the pleasure of the Crown. The Museum of Anthropology agreed to recognize the inherent rights of First Nations to control the representation of their own heritage and thus to give precedence to their moral interests over those of the government, a lending museum, or the archaeology profession. This recognition has not jeopardized the objects because the bands asked for higher standards of care than are currently in practice, nor has it limited the freedom of the curators to present the results of their research (though it did affect the manner of presentation).

Second, production of these two exhibitions extended far beyond their projected completion dates because of the consultation process. It takes time and patience to consult, especially when band representatives have many community responsibilities in addition to their ad hoc roles as museum advisors. To further complicate matters, some of the selected objects' excavation sites fell within the land-claim territories of neighboring band or tribal councils.

Third, the consultation process changes exhibition interpretation in matters of design as well as text. One of the primary concerns expressed by consultants was that both exhibitions be accessible to, and respectful of, those whose heritage they displayed, in addition to being accessible to non-Native visitors. In fact, the museum was asked to treat First Peoples as the primary audience for these exhibitions, something mainstream museums usually do not do because they are number-counters—exhibitions are constructed for the average museum visitor (usually non-Native), and to increase attendance and, therefore, make money.

The changes made as a result of this collaboration have been minor and subtle: a shift in expression here, a change in wording there, the choice of one background color over another, the choice of artifact and artifact mounts, and inspection of condition reports. The total effect for both exhibitions, in fact, *was* significantly different from what the curators and designers originally envisioned. The changes did not by and large regard questions of fact. The typical call was for clarification of exhibition text: What do you mean? How do you know that? Aboriginal representatives also requested the inclusion of a statement advocating the protection of cultural resources still in the ground and better preservation of excavated materials.

Coming to terms with the extended production timeline and the resulting changes in exhibition format created problems for the two exhibition teams. It was not just the challenge to their professional authority that mattered. It was difficult for individuals to accommodate the disruptions to their daily work routines caused by the open-ended nature of the consultation process and resulting deadline extensions. Future problems can be prevented if exhibition teams plan more flexible timetables.

This leads me to a final observation about these two archaeology exhibitions. Consultation properly begins at the outset of a proposal, not after an exhibition concept has been formulated or a schedule outlined. Also, it takes time to create and sustain a full partnership based on trust that may not have previously existed (at least to the degree required). If consultation is to be taken seriously, then consulting should be a main event for both sides.

Is There an Aboriginal Curatorial Prerogative?

I have discussed two broad types of non-Native curatorial perspectives, the transcendental and the contextual, and recognized that even within these types no two curators work alike. Beyond these differences, however, lies another potentially more profound possibility as to how museums represent First Peoples. I refer to individuals of Aboriginal descent curating Aboriginal art exhibitions.

What may have been a precursor of Aboriginal curatorship was a personal report I received about an exhibition of contemporary Mohawk art that appeared in a small Montreal gallery some years ago. Critics complained that the value of the exhibition was diminished because it included the less polished works of younger artists along with the more mature examples of established Mohawk artists. That was precisely the point of the show, according to its organizers; the established artists wanted to encourage younger members of their community by including them in the exhibition.

The differences between museum representations curated by people of Aboriginal descent and non-Aboriginals are probably matters of degree and not sharp divisions. Nevertheless, First Peoples argue that these distinctions are important and make a difference in such representations. Probably the most outspoken in this regard has been Alfred Young Man at the University of Lethbridge, Alberta.[12]

According to Doxtator's commentary in a catalogue for *Revisions,* the 1988 exhibition of Aboriginal art held at the Walter Phillips Gallery at the

Banff Centre for the Arts in Alberta, the primary differences between Aboriginal and non-Aboriginal interpretations are conflicting concepts of time:

> In western societies the idea of progress, based on the ever-increasing ingenuity of man, by implication judges the past to be very distinct from the present and, in many ways, inferior. The idea of the active interaction of the past with the present is not acceptable to western ideas of history, based as they are upon the differences between carefully measured units: centuries, decades, years, months, days and hours. Technology from a previous century is seen as obsolete and irrelevant to the present. Objects from the past are placed under Plexiglas in institutions where educational programs and museum interpretation must consciously create links between past and present. . . .
>
> In contrast, Indian writers and artists are constantly mixing and juxtaposing the past with the present because, from their viewpoints, it is the connections rather than the divisions that are important. Oral historical traditions do not concern themselves with precise units of time: they discuss the origins of the world, the meaning of a way of life, explanations of how things work. . . . [E]mphasis is placed not on the point of division or disruption between time periods but on the continuity between eras."[13]

Aboriginal curators, as well as Aboriginal artists, often do not perceive as important the common academic distinctions between anthropology and art history, art and artifact, art and craft, secular and spiritual, and aesthetics and politics. Their approach is more holistic or inclusive. The relationship between curator and artist also is different, with the Aboriginal connection being more holistic in interest and personal in tone when compared with the traditional curatorial relationship. This contrast becomes clearer if we formulate it in stereotypical or ideal-typical terms while still recognizing that in practice these differences may be less.

The traditional or mainstream curatorial prerogative, for example, could be said to begin with an impersonal, formalized or "objective" theoretical approach to art that is grounded in Western art history. Presumably, a curator working within this tradition would develop a professional and personal relationship with selected artists. On the other hand, considering

Gerald McMaster's relationship with Edward Poitras, Bob Boyer's with Allen Sapp, or Doreen Jensen's with Northwest Coast blanket-makers, one finds a reversal of priorities.[14] Though these curators (who are highly regarded artists as well) are no less skilled in methodology, connoisseurship, or intellectual sophistication, their personal relationships with the artists would seem to have preceded and transcended their more formalized curatorial interests. This is due in part to their shared experience of colonialism and socioeconomic marginalization, a kind of membership in an Aboriginal "communitas," to borrow Victor Turner's phrase.[15]

There is also a shared cultural experience. "It comes down to knowledge," Jensen said in reference to Bob Boyer's exhibition in 1994 of the works of Allen Sapp.[16] This knowledge is that of a curator sharing a common cultural background with the artist. In the case of Boyer and Sapp, they also share a common knowledge of the Cree language. Boyer was thus able to reach a far more intimate level of understanding of how Sapp's spiritualism and personal experiences are reflected in each of his works.[17] "Allen's work," Boyer stated in his catalogue essay, "is marked by his 'spiritual reverence' for the world and are [sic] not merely illustrations of the world around him. They are Allen's dreams of a past, present and, perhaps, a future."[18]

Aboriginal curators express a fundamental respect for the rights and interests of Aboriginal artists. They view Aboriginal artists as a whole people with distinctive histories and cultures, and recognize individual and cultural sovereignty. The exhibitors are not just artists who transcend their times and places, whose cultural backgrounds may be taken for granted, and whose works are to be displayed as individual pieces of art. Rather than imposing this Western curatorial perspective on Sapp's works, Boyer said he wanted to approach the exhibition from Sapp's point of view "because he's a friend of mine and I didn't want to do anything that was against my friend's values."[19] It is difficult to imagine a traditional curator admitting such sentiments in public—think of Norman Zepp's assertion that artists are not the best judges of their work. Perhaps they are not, but in this situation it seems to be more a question of whose interests are to take precedence, those of the curator or those of the artist.

When Jensen set out to interview blanket-makers for her *Robes of Power* exhibition in 1986, she said she did not make any presuppositions—she went to learn. "I asked only one question: 'What was your first experience with a button blanket?' And I listened. I didn't put in any ideas myself."[20] She taped and transcribed the interviews and sent them back to the blanket-

Fig. 15. Late Haida Elder Florence Davidson speaking at the opening of *Robes of Power*, 1986. Courtesy of the University of British Columbia Museum of Anthropology.

makers for approval, to "make sure that every informant has seen his or her material and is satisfied with its content"[21] (fig. 15).

Conclusions

The Task Force on the relations between museums and First Nations set out a comprehensive plan of action for Canadian museums. It was thought that voluntary compliance to recommendations mutually agreed upon by First Peoples and museum representatives would be more effective and less expensive than the legislative change brought about in the United States. The results so far, however, appear to be modest. There has been no lack of goodwill and intent on the part of museum individuals and First Nation communities, but there are structural factors that inhibit change. Museums are complex social organizations composed of intertwined layers of routines, obligations, schedules, and competing interests that frequently inhibit prompt or consistent responses to new initiatives. In addition, archaeologists, anthropologists, and art historians working in museums maintain allegiances to the traditions of their own professions, sometimes even at the expense of the interests of the institution that employs them. First Nations also have their sets of priorities and obligations.

A second problem with the Task Force recommendations is that many of them depend on government funding for implementation. In response to the recommendations, the Canadian government included Aboriginal initiatives on the list of projects eligible for museum funding. Several years later, it reduced the total amount of funding available to museums by forty percent.

A third problem, as Doxtator pointed out in her critique, is that the recommendations place the onus on museums to initiate change. Museums, like most formal organizations, tend to be conservative and have as a first priority self-perpetuation. Change is likely to be quicker and smoother when First Peoples take more active roles in their partnerships with institutions.

Presumably, Canadian museums will continue to employ First Peoples and to initiate different forms of consultation and collaboration. Differences in how First Peoples are represented in museum exhibitions, however, may require additional changes, including the revision of internal museum cultures and professions, and the traditional curatorial prerogative. Museums that increase the number of First Peoples curating their own exhibitions may be the most effective way of introducing these revisions.

NOTES

Note: I am indebted to Pam Brown, David Cunningham, Anne-Marie Fenger, Doreen Jensen, Charlotte Townsend-Gault, and Jennifer Webb for helpful discussions of topics presented in this paper, though they bear no responsibility for the final result.

1. What's in a name? Terms of self-reference and address change with the times. Though the Indian Act is still in force in Canada, the term "Indian" is widely disliked by the people the term is used to describe. "Native" (but not "Native Canadian") and "Aboriginal" are sometimes used in Canada as terms of self-reference and address; more commonly accepted at present are "First Nations" and "First Peoples." The accepted terms will be used interchangeably in this paper.

2. Tom Hill and Trudy Nicks, *Turning the Page: Forging New Partnerships Between Museums and First Peoples: Task Force Report on Museums and First Peoples*, 2d ed. (Ottawa: Assembly of First Nations and Canadian Museums Association, 1992), 7.

3. For the complete quotation, see Hill and Nicks, *Turning the Page*, 10. For the Nicks report, see Molly Lee, "Canadian Repatriation Update," *Anthropology Newsletter* 36, no. 8 (1995): 17.

4. Hill and Nicks, *Turning the Page*, 7.

5. Deborah Doxtator, "The Implications of Canadian Nationalism on Aboriginal Cultural Autonomy," in *Curatorship: Indigenous Perspectives in Post-Colonial Societies: Symposium Papers* (Victoria, British Columbia: University of Victoria, 1994), 21–22. Trained in museums and history, Doxtator, who conducted research on land claims, museum policies, and First Nations on behalf of the Royal Commission on Aboriginal Affairs, also worked as a consultant in the development of First Peoples curriculum resources and taught at York University in Toronto. She was a member of the Mohawk Nation, Ontario. Sadly, she died in 1998.

6. Repatriation was another important topic addressed in the Hill and Nicks Task Force report, and deserves a review in its own right.

7. Carol Duncan and Alan Wallach, "Museum of Modern Art as Late Capitalist Ritual: An Iconographic Analysis," *Marxist Perspectives* 1 (Winter 1978): 28–51; see also Carol Duncan, *Civilizing Rituals: Inside Public Art Museums* (New York: Routledge, 1995).

8. Janet Wolff, *The Social Production of Art* (New York: St. Martin's Press, 1981), 10.

9. A.L. Rees and Frances Borzello, eds., *The New Art History* (London: Camden Press, 1986).

10. All the information about this controversy is from Ray Conlogue, "A Curatorial Square-off," *Globe and Mail* (Toronto), 22 October 1994, sec. E, 5.

11. Conlogue, "A Curatorial Square-off."

12. See Alfred Young Man, "The Metaphysics of North American Indian Art," in *Indigena: Contemporary Native Perspectives*, eds. Gerald McMaster and Lee-Ann Martin (Vancouver and Toronto: Douglas and McIntyre in association with the Canadian Museum of Civilization, 1992), 81–99; Alfred Young Man, "Kiskayetum, a Painter of the Cree: The Co-existence of Non-contemporary Realities," in *Kiskayetum: Allen Sapp, a Retrospective*, ed. Bob Boyer (Regina: MacKenzie Art Gallery, 1994), 23–48; see also Michael M. Ames, "The Politics of Difference: Other Voices in a Not Yet Post-colonial World," *Museum Anthropology* 18 (3) (1994): 9–17.

13. Deborah Doxtator, "Reconnecting the Past: An Indian Idea of History," in *Revisions*, eds. Charlotte Townsend-Gault and Mary Anne Moser (Banff, Alberta: Walter Phillips Gallery in association with the Banff Centre for the Arts, 1992), 26–27.

14. See Edward Poitras and Gerald McMaster, "Installation artist Edward Poitras, Metis, conversation with museum director Gerald McMaster, Plains Cree." *Indian Artist* (Fall 1995), 106–11; Bob Boyer, "Introduction," in *Kiskayetum: Allen Sapp, a Retrospective*, ed. Bob Boyer (Regina: MacKenzie Art Gallery, 1994), 11–21; and Doreen Jensen and Polly Sargent, "Robes of Power, Totem Poles on Cloth," *Museum Notes* 17 (Vancouver: University of British Columbia Press and Museum of Anthropology, 1986).

15. Victor W. Turner, *The Ritual Process: Structure and Anti-Structure* (Chicago: Aldine Publishing, 1969).

16. Doreen Jensen. Interview by author; notes from a telephone conversation, 27 September 1995. Doreen Jensen is an artist, writer, curator, museum consultant, and member of the Git'ksan First Nation. For Boyer's work, see previous notes.

17. See Young Man, "Kiskayetum, A Painter of the Cree," in *Kiskayetum*, 34–37.

18. Boyer, "Introduction," *Kiskayetum*, 13.

19. Chris Dafoe, "Allen Sapp: Communicating on Canvas," *Globe and Mail* (Toronto), 16 January 1995, sec. A, 11.

20. Jensen, interview.

21. Jensen and Sargent, "Robes of Power," 4.

Learn About Our Past
to Understand Our Future:
The Story of the Mille Lacs Band of Ojibwe

JOYCELYN WEDLL

Introduction

I was born on the Mille Lacs Indian Reservation in east central Minnesota at a time when many changes were starting to take place in the lives of my people. We were moving from one-room tar-paper shacks to modern-day housing, and federal programs were coming to the reservation. I was greatly influenced by the tribal elders and leaders, who gave me a vision of the Anishinabe's future, and by my family. I would particularly like to pay tribute to my grandmother for caring for me physically, mentally, and spiritually. It is because of her guidance that I am able to share the story of my people, the Mille Lacs Anishinabe.

I will try to give you some understanding of who the Mille Lacs Band of Ojibwe are and how we worked together with the Minnesota Historical Society to plan and build our new museum. In telling the story of our people, it is necessary to offer a contemporary, as well as a historical, perspective. Both are crucial to an understanding of the people who make up the Mille Lacs Band of Ojibwe today.

The Mille Lacs Band of Ojibwe, like other Indian people who lived on the Mille Lacs Lake's shores in earlier times, developed a highly self-sufficient way of life. We found creative ways to use the resources of forest, marsh, and lake to sustain ourselves, and we built a rich tribal heritage that nurtured us through times of struggle and that still gives meaning to our lives today. We are a Woodlands people whose homelands are located near the lakes of the great northern forests and the headwaters of the Mississippi River. We are descendants of the Algonquian group, which originated on the east coast of North America.

The Ojibwe, coming from their homes around Lake Superior and farther east, entered the region around Mille Lacs Lake more than two centuries ago. Here my ancestors put down deep, strong roots that connect the human experience of countless generations and kept the spirit of tribal life flowing into contemporary times.

The Mille Lacs Indian Reservation was one of six reservations established for the Mississippi Ojibwe by federal treaty in 1855. In later years, the federal government pressured the Mille Lacs Ojibwe to move to a single, larger reservation at White Earth, Minnesota. Many members of the band resisted and, in the end, stayed on the reservation and in the region of the lake. The federal government's consolidation efforts arose because of pressure from non-Native settlers to access tribal lands, and also because of conflicts between tribal people and immigrants.

As a result of these conflicts, the federal government took away four of the six reservations established for the Mississippi Ojibwe. However, the Mille Lacs Band was given, through treaty, the unique status of "non-removable." Because Mille Lacs leaders had sought to prevent war and keep peace, the band was allowed to stay. Today we are a community well known for our understanding and use of tribal knowledge, customs, beliefs, and practices. We hold strong convictions about our right to live according to our own values and to provide the next seven generations with a meaningful living culture.

A sovereign tribal nation within the United States, the Mille Lacs Band is a member of the Minnesota Chippewa Tribe, a political confederation of six independent Chippewa reservations. We also share kinship with other Ojibwe bands in Wisconsin, Michigan, and Canada, along with cultural ties to many other tribal people throughout North America.

The Mille Lacs Band has an enrollment of 2,850 people. Our members live in several separate communities that are all part of the Mille Lacs governmental structure. During pre-Contact times, our ancestors supported themselves by hunting, fishing, and gathering. Not long after my people came into contact with the Europeans, the self-sufficient way of life we knew began to change.

Change and the Museum

The development of the Mille Lacs Indian Museum (fig. 16), which is located on the reservation, is part of the story of this change in our way of life. The museum began with Indian traders Harry and Jeannette Ayers, who came to the Mille Lacs area and settled near our reservation in 1919. The Ayers operated a trading post for some forty years, working with the Mille Lacs Band and developing a close relationship with the people. During their years at Mille Lacs, the Ayers collected a vast amount of cultural

Fig. 16. The Mille Lacs Indian Museum opened on 18 May 1996. Photo by Don Wedll.

material. In 1960, they donated the buildings, land, and materials they had collected at Mille Lacs to the Minnesota Historical Society (MHS). The partnership between MHS and the Mille Lacs Band, which has strengthened the programs and services offered by the museum, began at this time.

MHS's holdings of North American Indian cultural materials are among the strongest in the United States, and include the 1,400 artifacts collected by the Ayers. Described by ethnomusicologist Thomas Vennum as "one of the richest tribal treasures in the country," the Ayers collection includes tools and equipment used for traditional Ojibwe subsistence and recreational activities, numerous examples of traditional clothing, and hundreds of fine Ojibwe craft items (many of which were made for commercial sale). The Ayers's commercial ventures brought them into close association with Mille Lacs Band members, making the well-documented collection particularly valuable as a social history resource in addition to its usefulness for the study of Ojibwe aesthetic techniques.

The Mille Lacs Indian Museum has a unique status: it is a state historic site that also functions as a local history museum with active community participation. While the museum's administrative and financial support is provided by MHS, the history of the Mille Lacs Band is researched, interpreted, and brought to life by the people who know it best: Mille Lacs Band members.

Since the museum's inception, it has functioned as a meeting ground for a Native American community with a strong sense of its own heritage. This institution has drawn on the skills of local artisans who created many of the tools, utensils, toys, beadwork, and other items on exhibit. The collection also includes many excellent photographs documenting Ojibwe life in the Mille Lacs region during the nineteenth and twentieth centuries. Members of the Mille Lacs Ojibwe community are employed by the museum as administrators, tour guides, trading-post salesclerks, and craft demonstrators.

After a museum building was erected on the reservation site in 1960, the first of several teams composed of Mille Lacs members and Minnesota Historical Society staff developed its interpretive exhibitions. The Four Seasons Room, a diorama built and equipped by community members, remains the key attraction of the museum. This room is a life-size diorama exhibit that presents Ojibwe activities in each of the four seasons: hunting and spearfishing in the winter; processing maple sugar in the spring; gardening and berry picking in the summer; and harvesting wild rice in the fall.

Beginning with self-studies of the Mille Lacs site in 1979 and 1984, community members and MHS staff have worked with national consultants to describe our own experiences through exhibition development and intercultural communication. For two years, following a four-million-dollar appropriation from the State of Minnesota for a new museum building at Mille Lacs, a committee of MHS staff and Mille Lacs community members met regularly, first to plan the new museum building and then to develop a comprehensive interpretive program for the site.

The Indian advisory committee identified specific problems regarding the treatment of American Indian history in museums that should be addressed by Mille Lacs exhibitions. Two broad goals that emerged from these discussions influenced the development of exhibitions for the Mille Lacs Indian Museum. The first goal was to demonstrate that Indian people and their stories are not just part of the ancient past but are part of the present as well. The new Mille Lacs Indian Museum meets this goal by supplementing the view of traditional Ojibwe culture seen in the Four Seasons Room with new exhibitions displaying present-day stories of the Mille Lacs Band.

The second goal was to correct persistent stereotypes of Indian people and culture. The exhibitions meet this goal by offering first-person perspectives on historical events. Excerpts from interviews conducted by the tribal archives staff, along with additional interviews conducted for use in the exhibition, remind visitors that the people of Mille Lacs are individuals with specific perspectives on their community's history. People whose histories have long been interpreted by others tell their own stories in the Mille Lacs exhibitions.

The central exhibition message and supporting themes for these new exhibitions have been articulated and refined for at least ten years in discussions involving consultants, MHS staff, and Mille Lacs community members. The main exhibition message is that the Mille Lacs Band of Ojibwe has retained its culture, traditions, and its home for more than two centuries—often against great odds. Five themes in the exhibitions, outlined below, deliver this message.

Theme 1: Carrying culture through education and language

From approximately 1900 to 1940, many school-age children at Mille Lacs were forced to go to boarding schools in Pipestone, Minnesota; Flandreau, South Dakota; and Hayward and Tomah, Wisconsin. This policy, part of a nationwide attempt to assimilate Native Americans into the majority culture, caused vital elements of Ojibwe culture to be suppressed, discouraged, and thus rarely learned by several generations of Mille Lacs Band members. Students at boarding schools were routinely punished if they spoke their Native languages instead of English. At school, students were instructed to wear only European-derived clothing styles. At Mille Lacs, the traditional Midewiwin religion, already suppressed by Catholic and Protestant missionaries, was forced further underground as students were discouraged from practicing it.

Since the 1960s, the development of Ojibwe language skills and a culturally based school curriculum have been viewed as essential to reestablishing a community identity at Mille Lacs. The museum's exhibitions convey this emphasis in several ways. In a section on education, the telling experiences of several generations of a single family are described. At the reservation-based Nay Ah Shing School, where Ojibwe culture forms the core curriculum, many students are more fluent in their Native language and better versed in traditional activities than either their parents or grandparents.

In a listening booth devoted to the Ojibwe language, visitors can listen to Mille Lacs community members from several generations describe how and when they learned to speak Ojibwe, where they were able to speak it freely, and what it means for them to communicate with others in their Native language. Ojibwe can be heard in listening booths, and bilingual text appears throughout the exhibition, underscoring the centrality of the language in our culture (fig. 17).

Theme 2: Providing continuity through the evolution of traditional practices

The strongest evidence of cultural continuity at Mille Lacs is found in those areas most closely linked with the past. Traditional crafts and artifacts—

Fig. 17. Text panels feature Ojibwe and English throughout the exhibitions. Mille Lacs Indian Museum. Photo by Don Wedll.

birchbark baskets and canoes, beaded moccasins, dance outfits, bandolier bags, and quilled basketry—are often cited as examples of the community's strength and potential. The annual powwow, a traditional dance celebration, has become a community festival and reunion during which members gather for speeches given by tribal elders on such themes as dignity, community identity, and self-determination.

Expressions of this continuity are found throughout the exhibition. In many cases contemporary crafts are paired with their antecedents. Wherever possible, visitors are "introduced" to craftspeople through photographs along with personal comments on their work. The Mille Lacs Band's annual powwow is depicted as an event grounded in tradition but having great significance for today's members. Classes in basketmaking, beadwork, food preparation, and "lost arts," like black-ash basketry and mat weaving, are offered to community members who want to learn, relearn, or pass on valuable craft techniques.

Theme 3: Using kinship attachments as a defensive strategy

Stories of individual struggles to keep families, homes, and values intact in spite of upheaval, dislocation, and pressures for assimilation into the majority culture form the collective history shared by Mille Lacs Band members. Today, members refer to such individual stories to explain why close family relations among community members are highly valued and frequently discussed.

The importance of family ties to Mille Lacs community members is also demonstrated throughout the exhibitions. Introductory panels introduce visitors to community members by characterizing traditional Ojibwe clans as extended families. Subjects ranging from education and recreation to making a living are covered by focusing on the experiences of particular families. And on the exhibition timeline, the experiences of certain families are followed through history, chronicling their lives as part of a larger whole.

Theme 4: Defining community identity through a shared history of resistance

There is one important difference between the stories of many Indian nations and that of the Mille Lacs Band. While many nations were forced completely off their land by the United States government in the nineteenth century, the Mille Lacs Band managed to retain a tiny portion of its land base in central Minnesota. Today, members are proud that their ancestors refused to leave their homes on the lake. The non-removable status of the Mille Lacs Band is a frequent rallying cry in the State of the Band Addresses and other assertions of tribal identity.

Within the exhibitions, documentation of relocation attempts and resistance are found in two places. In one section, which focuses on the band's status as a sovereign nation, a listening station presents the words of leaders who negotiated treaties and other agreements with the United States government in the nineteenth century. Other components describe the tribal government structure and the treaty negotiations that led to the formation of the Mille Lacs Indian Reservation, and explain important concepts like sovereignty, non-removable status, self-governance, and self-determination. Profiles of individual leaders and their efforts are also included in the exhibition timeline.

Theme 5: Surviving through adaptation and flexibility

Throughout its history, the Mille Lacs Indian Reservation has experienced a relatively depressed economy with high unemployment. Work opportunities are limited and seasonal, and once-plentiful natural resources are now depleted. For the people of Mille Lacs, economic survival has meant piecing together a living from available opportunities, including tour guiding, farming, and logging, combined with resources garnered from gardening, processing wild rice, fishing, and hunting. In recent years, this pattern of subsistence living has eased somewhat, due largely to the opening of gaming facilities from which the band receives profits. Gaming establishments, the latest in a long series of opportunities seized by members in their struggle to stay afloat financially, have received mixed reviews at Mille Lacs. The presence of casinos has drastically reduced unemployment on the reservation and has provided funds for a high school, an elementary school, a clinic, a water tower, and our ceremonial buildings. There are many concerns, however, about the long-term effect of gaming on traditional values and community life.

The history of making a living at Mille Lacs is found in the first section of the exhibition. A listening station allows visitors to hear community members describe the range of occupations available to them over the years. Other exhibition components present a closer look at specific trades, including tourism, tradition-based activities like wild-rice processing, and a variety of businesses, such as gaming facilities, that have been operated by Mille Lacs Band members since the 1970s.

Broader Significance of the Museum

The history of the Mille Lacs Band of Ojibwe is a story of human life and culture in a particular place. It is also a tale with obvious and far-reaching significance, since common threads of history and culture tie it to a much larger Indian experience. In recent decades, scholars have analyzed this experience by using methods of ethnohistory, in which anthropological perspectives are applied to historical documentation. The goal of the ethnohistorian is to present a more complete and balanced picture of Native history and Indian-white relations, and to "remove American Indians from their traditional historical settings as silent props or ignorant pagans." Use of this method has led scholars, tribal historians, and exhibition developers to acknowledge multiple perspectives in their analyses of Native history, to consider events in nineteenth- and twentieth-century history from the viewpoint of tribal members, and to encourage members of Native communities to write or rewrite their own histories.

In recent years, scholars have begun to analyze the potential of various ethnohistorical methods in advancing general knowledge of American Indian history. In a recent article, historian Daniel Reicher warns that "although the subfield some call ethnohistory and others the New Indian History continues to flourish on its own terms, laments proliferate about its scant impact on larger areas of scholarship, on high school and college textbooks, and on the popular mind." Reicher goes on to describe examples of a "Euro-American popular consciousness" that prevailed during the Columbian Quincentennial in 1992, despite widespread efforts to present an evenhanded view of 1492.

The presentation of Indian history in museums can provide a response to the concerns of Reicher and the other scholars he cites. By definition, museum exhibitions reach a more diverse, general audience than do scholarly analyses. Through the incorporation of first-person narratives, live interpretations, and local examples of national trends, exhibitions can create an immediacy that compels visitors to remember and perhaps learn more about the subjects presented. Exhibitions can also grow and evolve in response to additional research or visitor inquiry.

Through the exhibitions at our museum, the voice of the Mille Lacs Band is heard. This goal, achieved through a combination of community consultation and original historical research, is an important one in view of recent trends in American Indian history, but is just as valuable to the Mille Lacs community itself. Throughout the twentieth century, but particularly during the last twenty years, the Mille Lacs Band has made significant progress toward achieving goals of self-determination and self-governance by (1) restructuring tribal government and justice systems, (2) establishing a tribal school with a core Ojibwe language and culture curriculum, and (3) undertaking a variety of business ventures.

The exhibition's title, *Learn About Our Past*, is taken from the 1989 State of the Band Address given by Tribal Chair Arthur Gahbow, in which he urged the people of Minnesota to study the history of the band as preparation for understanding current issues involving the use of natural resources. As is often the case with communities in the midst of economic and social change, members of the Mille Lacs community feel the need to explore and place current change in a historical context. In the words of elder James Clark, "We learn from what our history is, where we came from, where we're going. We also learn where we should be heading." In 1985, a comprehensive history of the Mille Lacs Band, *Against the Tide of American History: The Story of the Mille Lacs Anishinabe*, was published by the Minnesota Chippewa Tribe. In that same year, a successful oral history project was also established, and the Mille Lacs Tribal Archives was founded two years later. The new Mille Lacs Indian Museum takes this learning process a step further by presenting exhibitions in which members of the Mille Lacs Band are able to explore their own history while presenting it to others. When people walk into our museum, we want them to see that we are a community that is alive, vibrant, and growing, and not just something from the past. We want them to see that we are a community with a future in front of us.

FURTHER READINGS

Buffalohead, Roger. *Against the Tide of History: The Story of the Mille Lacs Band of Ojibwe.* Minnesota Chippewa Tribe, 1985.

Hill, Tom, and Trudy Nicks. *Turning the Page: Forging New Partnerships between Museums and First Peoples: Task Force Report on Museums and First Peoples.* 2d ed. Ottawa: Assembly of First Nations and Canadian Museums Association, 1992.

Martin, Calvin, ed. *The American Indian and the Problem of History.* Oxford University Press, 1987.

Parman, Donald L., and Catherine Price. "A Work in Progress: The Emergence of Indian History as a Professional Field," *Western Historical Quarterly* (1989).

Reicher, Daniel K. "Whole Indian History?" *William & Mary Quarterly* (1992).

United States West Research. *A Social History of Mille Lacs Peoples* (Fall 1993).

Appendices

Cultural Rethink

W. RICHARD WEST

It is time for the museum community to rethink how it reflects and addresses, interprets, and represents cultural diversity. Museums have the opportunity to become, on a far broader basis, engines of education and vital centers for the exchange of cultural ideas.

The National Museum of the American Indian (NMAI) is at the forefront of this museological shift from which there is no turning back. Its work reflects a strong belief that Indians are necessary to understanding, interpreting, managing, conserving, and exhibiting its unique collection of more than one million artifacts made by Indian people. The museum is committed to the Native perspective in every aspect of the way it functions—from the appointment of an Indian as director, to its insistence on exhibitions driven by the Native voice, and its willing involvement in repatriating museum objects to their original and rightful owners.

Repatriation calls for the return, upon request, of human remains and other culturally potent holdings to descendants or tribal groups who can demonstrate entitlement to the property. It is a powerful wake-up call for the American museum community, making it clear that contemporary Native peoples do not believe they are cultural relics of a dead or dying past. Rather, they are peoples and cultures of the present who draw upon ancient traditions and ways of being to survive in a vastly changed cultural landscape. This sense of continuum extends to a belief in the links between Native peoples and collections of their material culture in a number of the world's great museums. Under U.S. law, the reality of that link can mean that museums must return some of their holdings to Native communities. Far from being a threat to NMAI and its collections, repatriation is another way of entering into dialogue with the communities the museum serves.

Institutions such as NMAI, which hold the cultural patrimony of living Native peoples, must support Native communities in other culturally relevant ways as well. They must be proactive in making cultural material accessible to the peoples who still use it as an integral part of their lives.

The intellectual and spiritual realities Native peoples bring to cultural material differ, often profoundly, from the ways others may see the very same objects. Museums must be willing to confirm and validate the distinctions in cultural perspectives and realities between the Native and Western worlds by using the unfiltered Native voice systematically on the exhibition floor, in our public programming, and through new inclusive and collaborative approaches to scholarship. There is a kind of synergy at work here, whereby success in responding to the perspectives of Native peoples will ultimately benefit all visitors by giving them a fuller, richer, more genuine experience of the collection.

Part of this shift has to do with transforming museums from temples of an elite, privileged caste into places fostering multicultural dialogue. Much can be gained by painting interpretive canvases that give the new voices authority and authenticity.

NMAI's Cultural Resources Center, which opened in 1998 in suburban Washington, D.C., as the home for its collections, highlights the nature of the relationship between the museum and Native communities. The design was developed using Native architects, interior designers, and engineers to reflect the welcoming atmosphere characteristic of the Indian tradition of hospitality. As well as providing space for housing collections, the center includes an interactive library, conference rooms, and study areas. It will also provide space for the ceremonial and ritual care of cultural materials by Native Americans and will deliver cultural information to Native communities via a universal communications system intended to make the center a "virtual museum." It will liberate vast stores of human and material resources and share them across an equally vast physical space.

The three inaugural exhibitions at the museum's George Gustav Heye Center, which opened in New York City in 1994 (fig. 18), confirm the participation of Native voices in the interpretive process. *Creation's Journey: Masterworks from the National Museum of the American Indian* introduces and establishes the Native voice in the museum and shows the ways in which museums have used cultural objects in the past to present Indian cultures and peoples. Native songs, poetry, and commentary invite audiences to imagine the lives of the people who made the marvelous things on view.

For *All Roads Are Good: Native Voices on Life and Culture*, the museum invited twenty-three Native selectors from throughout the Western Hemisphere to explore its collections and choose and comment on works of cultural, spiritual, artistic, or personal significance.

Fig. 18. Opened in October 1994, the George Gustav Heye Center of the National Museum of the American Indian serves as an exhibition and education facility in New York City.

Finally, *This Path We Travel: Celebrations of Contemporary Native American Creativity* sought to demonstrate that Native cultural and artistic traditions continue through the hands, hearts, and spirits of contemporary artists. It featured the collective and individual talents of fifteen contemporary Native artists. Meeting over a three-year period at four different locations, participants experimented with the relationships between the Native and non-Native, traditional and contemporary. The exhibition, set up by the artists themselves, combined installation, sculpture, performance, poetry, music, and video.

The NMAI approach to interpreting culture has massive implications for the rest of the museum community.

Improving and increasing cultural representation is not merely a question of saying the same things we have always said to a more culturally diverse audience. More fundamentally, it is about bringing the diverse elements of cultural life into museums and allowing them to speak for themselves.

But this obligation to share cultural authority should not be considered the exclusive domain of ethnic institutions. Changing cultural demographics suggest that mainstream museums, historically Eurocentric in their outlook, need to foster the systematic inclusion of diverse cultural elements in their interpretive process.

If the museum community can make this cultural shift, museums have the chance to do even more than become centers for the exchange of cultural ideas. They will have the potential to assume a role that ascends to an entirely new plane—they will become far more pivotal to the continuing evolution of culture, and genuine instruments of the cultural reconciliation that society so desperately needs.

Reprinted, with changes, from *Museums Journal* 95 (June 1995): 30–31, published by the Museum Association, London.

The Indian in the Cabinet of Curiosity

RICHARD W. HILL, SR.

When museums first developed in this country, they looked upon Indian art as "artificial curiosities," mostly because Indian art was not considered fine art in the Euro-American tradition. Museums collected assorted oddities of exotic cultures that it was thought would soon disappear from the face of the earth. But the Vanishing American did not vanish. Indians have survived, and now it is the old ethnocentric notions about museums that seem to be vanishing. The new American museum has shifted its attitude, seeing Indians as part of an ongoing cultural matrix that adapts and adjusts to changing circumstances, yet remains uniquely "Indian" in the process.

Indians as Informants

This new relationship between Indians and museums has brought about changes in exhibitions, but persistent questions remain about who gets to tell the story. In the past, Indian cultures were seen as a resource from which objects were harvested for public consumption. Museums felt that if they discovered an Indian body in the ground, they could claim it for science. All objects made by ancient Indians were thought to belong to the archaeologist who discovered them. The dominant view was that Indian cultures were in varying stages of decay, and museums had to rush to preserve evidence of pre-Contact peoples. Museum curators, many of whom were academically trained anthropologists, looked at Indians as cultural informants. Indians provided information that was to be analyzed and verified by the non-Indian scholars to support or refute diverse theories about Indian origins, beliefs, and patterns of culture. The scholar was considered the expert in the telling of the Indian story.

Until a few years ago, Indian objects were regarded as anthropological specimens and were often part of natural history museums. In the most creative interpretations, life-size dioramas recreated a moment in time when Indians were considered "real" in the view of the museologists. More recently, Indians have been brought into museums as cultural presenters for new exhibitions. They have danced at openings and fundraising parties, demonstrated their skills as living exhibitions, and lectured on Native perspectives. Exhibitions in the last two decades, however, were still largely conceived and developed by non-Indians with the limited influence of Indian advisors.

Beyond Vanishing

Today's museums have begun to change the way they do business with Indians. There are more collaborations with Indians and, as a result, exhibitions are beginning to reflect more of the beliefs and values of the Indians themselves. Museums now look at Indians as constituents, not as exporters of material goods for study. The scope of exhibition curators has expanded to include educators, art historians, and exhibition developers whose thinking extends beyond anthropology. Indians serve as museum staff members or paid consultants on exhibition development teams. There remains a lack of Native curators in major institutions, but Native communities often have more direct ties to what gets shown, what gets said, and what happens in the museum.

Certainly the Native American Graves Protection and Repatriation Act has had an impact on this. Museums have been forced to rethink their relationship with Indians and to reassess their knowledge of their own collections. Objects are being reviewed to determine whether they are needed for Native rituals, proper to exhibit, or candidates for repatriation. The dust is being shaken off Indian objects that have languished on museum shelves for decades in search of new ways to demonstrate sensitivity to Native constituents. A quick review of current museum exhibitions shows that drastic changes have taken place.

New York State Museum in Albany opened its Mohawk longhouse exhibition in April 1988. This is the largest, most accurate Iroquois longhouse reconstruction in any museum. One unique feature is that visitors can walk right into the structure. Above, they can see men working on the pole frames as they extend the house. At one glass-enclosed end, a Mohawk family gathers around a winter fire to hear stories. The museum worked with Mohawk advisors to craft this scene and record stories, heard in Mohawk with an English interpretation. The simple use of a sparkling fire and overhead sound enhances the diorama's realism.

While some purists may feel that the trend toward museum animation is more Disney than educational, museums must determine the most effective ways to teach through exhibitions. Given the amount of money spent on such dioramas, museums may be about the least cost-effective way to teach, but increasing museum audiences indicate that more and more people are going to museums to learn about the world. The public is also seeking a negotiated truth; they understand that museums have biases, but they want to hear Native voices and get an Indian perspective on truth. So museums become a meeting ground, or at least a point of departure for most Americans who will never actually visit a Native community but want a sense of what life is like in the Indian world.

Back into the Cabinet

The life-size diorama is the magnet that pulls the audience into that story. In many cases the dioramas are wonderfully appointed, with sharp attention to details, extremely lifelike figures, and beautifully painted backgrounds that capture a glimpse of the past. But the dioramas are in themselves a throwback to the old-style museums that freeze Indians in the past. The drama of the diorama as a lighted box full of wonderful things is not much different from the old cabinets of curiosity that graced upper-class Victorian parlors. The cabinets held Indians at a safe distance, capturing the essence of their expressions but taking them completely out of context and out of Indian control. The diorama becomes a big toy for adults, allowing all to play Indian for a moment in time. Visitors join the scene and wonder what it must have been like. But wonder is all we can do.

Interestingly, the dioramas in Albany contain no original objects. Everything is a replica. Apparently the museum decided not to show real objects, and had non-Indians replicate known objects and conjecture on what the rest may have looked like. Strangely, the diorama is evidence of the craftsmanship of non-Indians rather than Indians. It is a three-dimensional theory about Indian life, but museum visitors perceive it as gospel truth. Impressions created by staring into a large diorama full of Indians can last a lifetime.

So what do such dioramas tell us about Indians? Most challenging are representations of ancient Indians, which are at best a good guess. The cut of the clothing, designs on clothing, and hairstyles are all conjectures. Yet dioramas remain a popular museum tool, and the supposed realism of the scene helps to place us within another time, another place, and another world view.

Aboard the Starship Indian

The Los Angeles County Museum of Natural History utilizes full-scale life-cast figures in different ways. There are older exhibitions of Indian figures within historic landscapes, but there are also mannequins of contemporary

Indians. Four Zuni women dressed in traditional clothing with water jars on their heads are part of one exhibition. These women look as if they have walked right out of the Gallup Inter-Tribal Ceremonies and into the museum, smiling and talking among themselves all the way. They seem more human than the mannequins engaged in hunting, gathering, and trading activities often depicted in dioramas. These women have personalities, yet they are standing in the middle of a large glass case, surrounded by examples of Pueblo pottery. There is no landscape, no household scene—simply the figures, standing as if they were beamed aboard a starship.

The Milwaukee Public Museum installed an exhibition called *Tribute to Survival,* which has an eerie diorama. A small circle of modern powwow dancers moves strangely around and around, like a cultural carousel, each dancer frozen in a movement of the dance. Overhead sound brings the music of the drum, bells of the dancers, and the words of the M.C., who is visible off to the side of the dancers. These are some of the most lifelike figures I have ever seen in a museum—their eyes seem to watch you as they pass along, and the attention to facial details, different colors and styles of hair, and contemporary dance outfits is impressive—yet the rotating dancers, silent and motionless, seem just the opposite of a real powwow.

The exhibition designers incorporated motion in a couple of figures that spin in place and used light to dramatize the dancers as they enter the dance circle at the powwow's grand entry. As a masterwork of museology, this is quite extraordinary, but the diorama is a weak interpretation of the movement, sounds, and powerful emotions of dance. Even more disappointing is that none of the models are named in the exhibition. They are listed as types of dancers, not as individuals who have come together to dance. This lack of proper identification further dehumanizes the figures.

Across from this new diorama is an older scene of two Plains Indian men riding on horseback as they chase down some buffalo. This diorama captures the drama of the buffalo hunt, the power of the animals, the tension of the horses, the skill of the riders, and the sense of excitement as the moment of truth is at hand. It is a large diorama with a panoramic view, with no glass separating the viewer from the figures. It is hard to explain its appeal. Perhaps it is our collective romantic view of the chase. Together, this scene and the newer powwow exhibition help to create a fuller view of Indian life. Interestingly, I noticed that children spent more time looking at the older scene than they did the animated one.

The Field Museum of Chicago installed a life-size earthlodge several years ago. At first glance it appears to be a spaceship that landed right in the middle of the museum. Atop the earthlodge are several figures representing Pawnee Indians, wrapped in blankets, staring at museum visitors as they approach the exhibition. When the exhibition first opened, people could walk right inside. The interior was finished off like an actual earthlodge and people could sit on the buffalo robes and see household goods as they may have appeared in the historic setting. There were no mannequins inside the lodge. Overhead, a voice told of the traditions of the earthlodge.

Apparently, according to one of the guards, when the voice came on it scared the living daylights out of people—especially the children—who were inside. I tried to figure out why people were so frightened. When I looked at the figures in the earthlodge, I found my answer: they actually look like zombies, with stark eyes and emotionless expressions. They are a bit scary. A gate had to be installed across the opening to keep the visitors out, but when I visited the same exhibition recently I was pleased to see that guided tours are now being offered inside the earthlodge at special times. The overhead voice has been silenced, and people seem not to be afraid any more.

Out of the Display Case and into the Future

Will museums forever associate Indians with dioramas containing life-size figures? Will museum visitors always expect to see casts of Indians next to the stuffed animals, mechanical dinosaurs, and replicated fauna? Are there more effective ways through which we can animate the lives of Indian peoples who often live far from the museums?

Dickson Mound Museum in Illinois tries a bold new approach that I found more satisfying. This notorious site sits on an actual grave mound where, in the past, visitors could see the exposed remains of nearly three hundred dead Indians. For decades it was a popular tourist attraction, but protests eventually prompted the state to take over the site and construct a new facility over those exposed graves.

The exhibition designers, Gerald Hilferty and Associates of Athens, Ohio, approached that sacred space with a healthy mixture of respect and creativity. Instead of building exhibitions over the graves, they created a large dark room with a ramped walkway around the perimeter. In this way no one walks over the graves, which are covered over in a tomb. The designers then hung white scrims and cords from the ceiling and stretched other scrims over the floor. Using light and recordings of winds and other sounds, they project images on these scrims that create a sense of the world view of the ancient ones from that site.

Multiple images based on actual artifacts and petroglyphs were combined with scenes of the land, sky, clouds, waters, and people's hands at work planting, nurturing, and harvesting the crops. The soundtrack combines natural sounds with the spoken word to animate the images. All of the text was taken from actual speeches, songs, and prayers offered by Indians themselves. The powers of the Native universe come alive in that space. The exhibition is an extension of Indian beliefs that allows the visitor to experience Native world views with the kind of emotions necessary to transcend science. The designers used life-size figures illuminated from time to time during the fifteen-minute production. In my opinion, this is less effective: the exhibition's message is powerful without any need for characterization. Upon exiting the space at the lower levels, visitors meet contemporary Indians in photo panels that show that, although life has changed, the ideas of the ancient ones are still alive in this generation of Indians.

It was at Dickson that I finally felt that a museum had captured the sense of the people. Somehow I sensed that the ancestral spirits of those Indians laid to rest at that spot would be pleased by the presentation and pleased to know that Indians are still here, still believing in the same ideas, and still practicing the same cycles of thanksgiving. That exhibition helped me feel even more connected to the ones who lived here before.

Reprinted, with changes, from *Native Americas* 12 (Winter 1995): 58–61, published by the Akwe:kon Press, American Indian Program, Cornell University.

Contributors

MICHAEL M. AMES, professor of anthropology and director of the Museum of Anthropology at the University of British Columbia, has conducted research in Ceylon and India, and with Euro-Americans, Asian Americans, and Native Americans in the United States and Canada. He is particularly interested in how the diversity of culture can be adequately represented within the context of public institutions like museums.

JANICE CLEMENTS (Warm Springs Tribe of Confederated Tribes of Warm Springs) is a member of the board of directors of the Museum at Warm Springs in Oregon and travels throughout the country to promote the museum. An accomplished beadworker, she sews traditional clothing and dance outfits. Ms. Clements is actively involved in her community and well respected for her teachings on the culture and traditions of her people.

RICHARD W. HILL, SR. (Tuscarora) is an associate professor at State University of New York at Buffalo. He was formerly special assistant to the director of the National Museum of the American Indian. His essays and photographs on Native American life have been widely published.

EVAN M. MAURER is director and CEO of the Minneapolis Institute of Arts. He was a professor and director of the University of Michigan Museum of Art in Ann Arbor. In 1977, as curator of the department of Africa, Oceania, and the Americas at the Art Institute of Chicago, he produced *The Native American Heritage: A Survey of North American Indian Art.*

JAMES D. NASON (Comanche), professor of anthropology and director of the American Indian Studies Center at the University of Washington in Seattle, is also a curator for the Thomas Burke Memorial Washington State Museum. His areas of specialization are Native North America and Micronesia.

DAVID W. PENNEY is curator of Native American art at the Detroit Institute of Arts and adjunct professor of art history at Wayne State University. He has been project director of numerous exhibitions, among which are *Images of Identity: American Indians in Photographs, Art of the American Indian Frontier: The Chandler-Pohrt Collection, Ancient Art of the American Woodland Indians,* and *Lords of Sipan.*

JOYCELYN WEDLL (Mille Lacs Band of Ojibwe) is director of the Mille Lacs Indian Museum. She has been involved with all aspects of the newly built museum, from selection of the architect and development of the building design to development of exhibitions that focus on the Mille Lacs Band's social, economic, and legal concerns.

W. RICHARD WEST (Southern Cheyenne and member of the Cheyenne and Arapaho Tribes of Oklahoma), as founding director of the National Museum of the American Indian, Smithsonian Institution, has supervised the architectural process and program planning for the museum. Prior to his appointment as director of the museum, he was partner in an Indian-owned law firm. He has devoted his professional and much of his personal life to working with Native Americans on cultural, educational, legal, and governmental issues.

PHOTOGRAPH CREDITS

The photographers and the sources of illustrative material are as follows, with copyright in the name of the photographer or source.

Fig. 1:	The Minneapolis Institute of Arts
Fig. 2:	Bibliothèque Nationale, Paris
Fig. 3:	The British Library
Fig. 4:	The Brooklyn Museum
Fig. 5:	Smithsonian Institution, National Museum of the American Indian
Figs. 6–8:	James Nason
Fig. 9:	Beth Russell
Fig. 10:	The Museum at Warm Springs
Fig. 11:	Olney Patt, Jr.
Figs. 12–15:	The University of British Columbia Museum of Anthropology
Figs. 16–17:	Don Wedll
Fig. 18:	Museums Association, London

Index

The changing presentation
of